Contents

1   **Some mark to make, some word to tell**
3   Purposes and background of this book
8   Enriching literacy – ten maxims underlying this book

11   **Repertoire, confidence, juggling, winning: aspects of personal and bilingual identity**
14   An extensive repertoire: *Thaeba*
15   Keen to communicate meaning: *Mohammed*
17   Juggling all the time: *Usha and Lena*
18   'I won': *Andreia*
20   Becoming and being bilingual: *some points arising*

23   **Places to go, things to do: routes for bilingual learners**
25   Key Visuals – *access through seeing*
34   Collaborative Groupwork – *the campaign for real communication*
42   Frames and Frameworks – *skeletons and scaffolds to help children write*
46   Ways with Words – *meanings, nuances and power*

49   **Tales and texts to inspire and empower**
50   Universal themes in the subject-matter
52   Characters and cultural milieu
54   Richness and quality of language
55   Ambiguity, humour and links

59   **Whole-school policies: reviews, reflection and renewal**
60   Practical classroom methods
63   Management and organisation
64   Partnership teaching
65   Welcoming new arrivals
66   Curriculum for a just and inclusive society

69   **References, bibliography and useful addresses**

Acknowledgements

Background

This book was compiled from material developed at a range of inset courses and projects organised by Brent Language Service in 1996/98, and funded under the Grants for Educational Support and Training (GEST) scheme of the Department for Education and Employment. The GEST programme in Brent was managed by a partnership involving headteachers, the inspection service and the language service. Its members were Kim Beat (Head of Barham School), Lakshmi De Zoysa (Head of Brent Language Service), Rose Ive (Inspector for English), Lynwyn Jones (Head of Lyon Park Infants School), Melissa Loosemore (Head of Roe Green Junior School) and Kawal Singh (Head of Gladstone Park School).

Keynote lectures which were particularly influential in relation to material in this book were given on theoretical approaches by Jim Cummins (Ontario Institute of Studies in Education) and on key visuals and collaborative learning by Martin Cortazzi (University of Leicester) and Steve Cooke (Resource Centre for Multicultural Education, Leicester). Tutors and organisers from Brent Language Service included Lakshmi De Zoysa, Shobhana Devani, Janina Falczynska, Jo Melhuish and Mo Strangeman. From outside Brent the lecturers included staff from the Open University, Thames Valley University, University of Reading and University of London Institute of Education.

The main body of the book derives from a course entitled *Language and Literacy in Multilingual Schools – developing our expertise as trainers and leaders*, led by Robin Richardson, co-director of the Insted educational consultancy and formerly director of the Runnymede Trust.

Administrative support for the courses was provided by Kiran Kakad, Shantilal Patel, Sanjaya Siriwardena and Paul Wildish.

Editorial

The book was compiled and edited by Robin Richardson, in consultation with an editorial group whose members were Sue Browne (Sudbury Junior School), Lakshmi De Zoysa (Brent Language Service), Maureen Price (Carlton Vale Infants School), Chris Raeside (John Kelly Girls' Technology College) and Mo Strangeman (Brent Language Service).

General

In addition to the editorial committee, mentioned above, many individual teachers in Brent – both in mainstream schools and in the language service – contributed ideas, directly or indirectly, to this book. Several of them are acknowledged by name on page 70. We are grateful to them, and are grateful also to friends, contacts and colleagues in other language services around the country for their moral and professional support over many years.

Publisher and design

We are grateful to Trentham Books for their partnership, advice and assistance in matters of design, printing, publishing and distribution. The cover design is by Aquarium Graphic Design.

Additional copies

Additional copies of this book are available from Brent Language Service, c/o Centre for Staff Development, Brentfield Road, London NW10 8HE, telephone 0181 937 3370, or directly from Trentham Books (see page 72). There are reduced prices for bulk orders of 10 or more copies.

Some mark to make, some word to tell

Shortcuts

The figures, charts and tabulations in this book are convenient shortcuts to the book's principal concerns and ideas. They are as follows:

Figure 1:   Overlaps between four main kinds of learning *(page 7)*

Figure 2:   Examples of four types of language use *(page 22)*

Figure 3:   Routes for bilingual learners *(page 24)*

Figure 4:   Developing and using a key visual *(page 27)*

Figure 5:   Differences between everyday English and curriculum English *(page 34)*

Some mark to make, some word to tell

Purposes and background of this book

Into the world

Children come into the world, said the poet Langston Hughes, 'like stroke of lightning in the night'. And they come, he added, with:

> Some mark
> To make
> Some word
> To tell.

This book

This book is about making marks and telling words – literacy and oracy, texts and talk.

To be empowered

To write is to 'tell your word'. If children can both write and tell their word they can make their mark in other ways as well, for they can play a fuller part in the wider world around them. The marks they put from time to time on voting slips at elections, for example, will be of a piece with contributing actively to political, economic and cultural affairs. We have compiled this book because we want bilingual children in British schools to be empowered in their writing and telling, and therefore empowered to make their mark in a wide range of other ways as well.

Birth

Oh, fields of wonder
Out of which
Stars are born,
And moon and sun
And me as well,
Like stroke
Of lightning
In the night
Some mark
To make
Some word
To tell.
Langston Hughes

Langston Hughes' poem 'Birth' was first published in *Fields of Wonder*, New York 1954. It has recently been re-printed in *My Song is Beautiful: poems and pictures in many voices*, selected by Mary Ann Hoberman, Little, Brown and Company 1994.

Her mark

Kristien Müller describes voting in the South African elections, 1994:

I scuttle into my booth. It is very quiet in here. It's like entering a shower cubicle. I feel like throwing back my head to catch the stream on my upturned face, to feel my whole body laved by it. The water of history ... How lucky I am to be able, at last, to vote *for* something, not just against ... We're all here together ... all our bodies exposed to the exuberant stream that splashes over us, cleansing us, confirming us even as we make our cryptic crosses ... Here is my cross. Kristien Müller, her mark.

Imaginings of Sand by André Brink, 1996

Background

This book arises from teachers looking in fine detail at how children learn to use English as an additional language, in both speech and writing. We attended to the children's strengths and skills as well as to their problems and difficulties. We then tried out various ways of helping them. We describe in this book some of the things which seemed to work best, and reflect on what we learnt. We hope the book will be a useful practical resource in primary schools throughout Britain, particularly at this time in educational history when literacy is receiving much emphasis from the government but when the distinctive needs, strengths and skills of bilingual children seem to be largely ignored in official policy.

Gratitude

The book has its origins in one particular local education authority, and most immediately it draws on the ideas and practical experience of teachers and headteachers in this particular place. We are grateful to the many close colleagues, both in the language service and in schools, who have contributed suggestions and ideas to these pages, and without whom the book could not have been created. Also, we are grateful to friends, colleagues and contacts in other places – schools, language services, higher education – around the country. We hope that they will readily recognise, as they read through these pages, that we have learnt from them and have been inspired by them. We see the book as belonging to, and inspired by, teachers, headteachers and lecturers throughout Britain, not just by those in one locality.

Enrichment

The term 'enriching' in our title is both an adjective and a verb:

- **Adjective:** literacy is enriching, empowering and fulfilling for each individual child.

- **Verb:** official policy on literacy needs to be enriched and enlivened by careful and respectful attention to the bilingualism which is a key feature of the vast majority of urban schools.

Summary of contents

The book has four main sections –

- **Repertoire, confidence, juggling, winning: aspects of personal and bilingual identity**

  We introduce some children and young people who are bilingual. We wish here to stress the complexity and diversity of bilingualism, and wish also to foster respect and admiration for it. In our comments on points arising we recall familiar distinctions between 'everyday language' and 'curriculum language', and between low and high levels of cognitive challenge.

- **Places to go, things to do: routes for bilingual learners**

  We focus here on three main types of practical classroom activity – the use of visual material to express and communicate key ideas ('key visuals'), the use of collaborative groupwork to provide opportunities for genuine communication between children and between children and teachers, and the use of writing frames to develop competence in 'curriculum language', as distinct from 'everyday language'. We stress throughout the importance of high cognitive challenge, and of attending to bilingual children's distinctive needs and strengths.

- **Tales and texts to inspire and empower**

  We suggest a range of questions which colleagues should ask when reviewing the stocks of fiction and poetry at their schools and in their classrooms. In particular we are interested in stories which have rich and resonant language, which handle universal themes in their subject-matter, and which are accessible and inclusive in their choice of characters and cultural contexts. These are the kinds of text which bilingual children, and indeed all children, need to know and enjoy.

- **Review, reflection and renewal: questions for whole-school policy**

  We summarise our conclusions and recommendations in the form of a series of checklists. We hope that these checklists will be useful at inset sessions, and for planning, auditing and evaluation. They are concerned not only with specific aspects of language development but also with the overall context (including the curriculum) in which language development takes place.

Uniqueness and abstraction

The book starts by attending to some young people, Thaeba, Mohammed, Usha and Lena, and Andreia. They are not supposed to be 'typical' or 'representative', other than in the obvious but vital sense that every child is a unique individual, just as these young people are. Every child has their own unique and complex ways of using language and languages, and of developing their own unique identity in relationships with others – their parents and family, their friends and peers, their teachers and school.

We hope that our descriptions of some specific and unique people will stimulate our readers to compile broadly similar profiles of the children whom they teach, and to see their children as whole persons with unique features, not just as – as the rather awful terms so often, alas, are – 'EAL pupils' or 'Section 11 pupils'.

Every child is, yes, unique. But teachers necessarily approach their pupils with certain general principles and assumptions in mind. These are inherently abstract rather than specific. An abstraction frequently used in this book involves insisting that the learning of English as an additional language cannot be, and must not be, divorced from three other kinds of development – (a) academic, (b) cognitive and (c) personal and social. The inter-relationships and overlaps can be pictured in a simple diagram, as in Figure 1 opposite.

Ten maxims

In order to explain the ideas in this diagram in greater detail, we have drawn up a set of ten maxims. These are shown on the next pages. They are none of them particularly surprising or controversial. Nearly everyone using this book, we expect, will readily agree with them. Yet at a national level, relatively few of them appear in debates about school improvement and school effectiveness, and they do not seem to be adequately stressed in the National Literacy Strategy. It is timely and appropriate, therefore, to articulate them, even at the risk of re-stating the obvious.

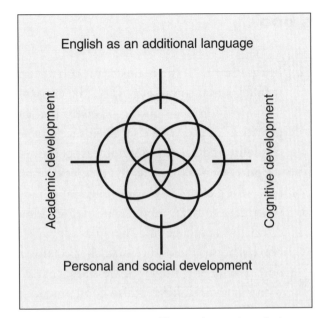

English as an additional language

Academic development

Cognitive development

Personal and social development

Figure 1: overlaps between four main kinds of learning

Your view

Before looking at our list of maxims (pages 8-10), you may like to pause and wonder what *you* would put in such a list. In the light of your own work in multilingual classrooms and schools over the years, what would you say are the ten or so most important things you have learnt – the ten most important principles which in your view should guide schools into the future, the ten most important points for the staff of a school to agree on?

Then compare your list with ours.

- What have we left out?

- What, if anything, have we included that you disagree with?

Throughout these pages we hope you will discuss and argue with us. Out of such joint reflection amongst teachers there will be benefits for children. For children will be better able, to quote Langston Hughes again, to make their mark, and to tell their word.

Enriching literacy – ten maxims underlying this book

1 'Only connect ...'

It used to be widely thought that children not proficient in English should *first* be taught English and only then should learn other subjects. For this reason they were put in special language centres or classes. Such centres and classes no longer exist, and the assumptions underlying them have been totally discredited. But there is still a need to integrate and connect the acquisition of English more closely with other kinds of learning – in particular with:

- **academic development**, i.e. progress in the subjects of the national curriculum

- **cognitive development**, for example generic intellectual skills of observing, sequencing, categorising, predicting, hypothesising, reasoning, and so on

- **personal and social development**, for example personal qualities such as self-confidence and self-esteem, pride in being bilingual, and social skills in interaction with other children.

Figure 1 on page 7 recalls visually that these various kinds of learning should go hand in hand. With regard to a piece of 'EAL' teaching it is seldom if ever sufficient to ask only about the linguistic structures and vocabulary which children are expected to learn. Teachers should also consider the generic cognitive processes in which the children are involved, the academic knowledge and understanding which they are acquiring, and the personal and social skills and attitudes which they are developing.

2 Integration with the mainstream curriculum

It follows that so far as possible the curriculum provided for bilingual children should be precisely the same as that which is provided for everyone else. Their teachers need special expertise, certainly, and need to provide particular kinds of assistance and support ('scaffolding', as the technical term sometimes is), such that – for example – the meanings of unfamiliar words are clear from the context, and such that children learn to use the distinctive language of different academic subjects. Much of this book is about the nature of such specialised assistance and support. Frequently, however, we show that what is good practice with bilingual children is also good practice for all other children as well.

3 Partnership

It follows also that there needs to be a genuine partnership between specialist teachers on the one hand and mainstream teachers on the other. Neither can achieve on their own what needs to be done. Specialists need levels of expertise and understanding which most mainstream teachers do not have. At the same time mainstream teachers need to accept that they have a major responsibility for fostering bilingualism. They cannot leave everything to a support teacher, however well-qualified and expert the support teacher may be. Most of the specific examples in this book derive directly from partnerships working well.

4 The need for whole-school policies

Teaching English as an additional language is a matter for a whole school, and needs to be integrated with several other policies – particularly, of course, with policies for English and language, and policies about teaching methods, assessment and classroom organisation. It is the headteacher and governing body who are responsible for overall policy, and who are responsible for ensuring that all teachers accept that supporting children learning English as an additional language is part of their professional task, and that all are given practical guidance and appropriate training.

5 The essential importance of talk

Most children, like indeed most adults, learn to write well as part of a process of learning to engage in purposeful talk. They therefore need to be given tasks which require them to think aloud, to argue, to justify and to negotiate, and at the same time to increase their vocabulary by having to use specialist terms and concepts. For this reason collaborative groupwork is a necessity, not – as its critics sometimes seem to suppose – a mere distraction.

6 The essential importance of writing

All pupils and students in schools need to be able to use in writing the distinctive genres and terminology of the main academic subjects. There is no other way of achieving success in public examinations. There is frequently a big gap, however, between children's oral abilities on the one hand and their writing skills on the other. This gap is often particularly wide in the case of pupils for whom English is an additional or alternative language. Focused attention therefore needs to be given to improving writing skills.

7 The role of parents

In the field covered by this book, as in most other fields of education, parental involvement is essential. We give several examples of close working relationships with parents. Parents of bilingual children have vital knowledge about their children which schools need to have also, and can work in partnership with schools in a wide range of ways if they are warmly and genuinely invited to do so.

8 Bilingualism

Throughout this book we take it for granted that children should be encouraged to maintain and develop their home and community languages, and should be encouraged to use these languages as vehicles for learning. Proficiency in English is vitally important for them, certainly, but there is absolutely no reason why such proficiency should be attained at the expense of losing their first language, or through their first language being de-valued. On the contrary, bilingualism properly recognised is a positive benefit to cognitive development, and therefore to proficiency in two or more languages.

9 Identity

To be bilingual is to have a dual identity. It is important that the multiple affiliations and loyalties of bilingual children should be recognised and respected. This involves knowing and caring where, as the phrase is, 'they are coming from'. Also, equally important, it involves knowing and caring 'where they are going to' – their future as British citizens whose sense of personal and cultural identity will include belonging to two or more different, though intermingling, cultural traditions.

10 Racism, exclusion and prejudice

In terms of ethnicity, as also in terms of class, Britain is an unequal society. People who have their origins in Africa, the Caribbean and South Asia are not as involved as white people in mainstream economic, social and political life, and they frequently meet prejudice and discrimination, and sometimes harassment or even violence. The racism they face has two main strands – (a) 'colour racism', where the markers of difference and grounds for negative discrimination are to do with physical appearance, particularly skin colour, and (b) 'cultural racism', where the grounds for hostility and exclusion are to do principally with language and religion. To care about the advancement of bilingual children in British schools involves strenuously addressing both main strands of racism, and both in schools and in wider society.

Repertoire, confidence, juggling, winning: aspects of personal and bilingual identity

Richness

In order to create the descriptions of Thaeba and Mohammed, the teacher worked directly with the two children on a variety of tasks in different areas of the curriculum, and took opportunities to ask them about their language skills, home lives and personal interests. In addition he made a point of watching them in a fly-on-the-wall style across a range of situations, including structured desk activities, small groups, paired work, one-to-one with the class teacher, the home corner and the playground. Further, he talked informally with parents and with older brothers and sisters, and consulted the school's admission forms.

"Compiling these profiles of Thaeba and Mohammed," wrote the teacher (Frank Williams) later, "proved to be a really enlightening experience. I learnt not only a great deal about these two children in particular but also about aspects of the experience and background of many of the other children at our school.

"The most striking feature that came to light was the richness of the language experience of the children. Neither Thaeba nor Mohammed is 'bilingual', for both use more than two languages each – they can operate effectively in three different languages, albeit with differing degrees of competence, in real communicative contexts.

"Though similar to each other in their multilingual proficiency, the two children are significantly different in their circumstances. The one belongs to a family which is well established in London and to a community to which the majority of the children in our school belong. Her family came to Britain by choice for economic reasons, and they see their future here. The other belongs to a family which has suffered an unimaginable dislocation in its circumstances, which is isolated from its roots and culture, and is suffering a dramatic decline in wealth and status. It does not take for granted that its future is in Britain."

Repertoire, confidence, juggling, winning: aspects of personal and bilingual identity

Introductory notes

We introduce here a number of young people. We have several different purposes in mind:

- to recall the complexity and diversity of bilingualism – no two bilingual children are the same

- to foster respect and admiration for bilingualism, and for the outlooks, attitudes and skills which bilingual children have

- to suggest that all specialist teachers of English as an additional language – and many mainstream teachers too, incidentally – should undertake the kinds of simple observation and enquiry on which these descriptions are based

- to introduce some general points about bilingualism and the learning of English as an additional language.

Two of the descriptions were written by a specialist EAL teacher in an infants school. The headteacher was in no doubt that time spent on compiling such detailed profiles would be of great practical benefit both to the specialist and to the class teachers, and would in due course feed into valuable school-based inset. The third description is from a transcript of young people recalling how they learnt English, and talking about the pleasures of being able to switch back and forth between languages and between cultures. The fourth is similarly about a secondary school student. It vividly illustrates the ways in which learning an additional language is bound up with issues of personal and cultural identity, and with everyday personal relationships.

An extensive repertoire: Thaeba

Family

Thaeba is four years old, the youngest of four children all born in London. Her parents came to Britain fifteen years ago from the Punjab region of Pakistan. Her father works for the Post Office and her mother is the main carer of the children – the other three children in the family are aged 12, 11 and 7. All Thaeba's grandparents still live in Pakistan, but they visit the UK regularly. Thaeba visited Pakistan when she was one year old and may go again next year. All her family are practising Muslims and maintain strong ties with the local Pakistani community.

Repertoire

Thaeba already has an extensive repertoire of languages. Her mother reports that Urdu is the first language of the home. Thaeba speaks to her parents in Urdu and enjoys watching Urdu videos and Asian channels on cable TV. (The spoken Urdu used in most films, by the way, is virtually identical to Hindi.) Her brother Gulyaman, aged seven, says that he and Thaeba talk together in Panjabi and English, and names Panjabi as his strongest language. He readily speaks Panjabi in class with his friends.

School

At school Thaeba uses English almost exclusively. The only times I have heard her use anything other than English have been when I myself have greeted her with 'Salaam o alaikum' and she has given the standard reply (usually with a giggle), and when she gave a brief answer in Urdu when addressed in Urdu by the school welfare officer, Mrs Khan. I have watched her closely when she is talking with friends of the same linguistic background as herself and have noted that she always speaks English even when addressed by her friends in Panjabi or Urdu. Her best friend Aysha happily uses Urdu in class, when asked, for counting and naming things. Thaeba will smile but cannot be persuaded to join in. Further, she never code-switches. If she does not know a word in English she simply points at an object or asks what it is.

It would be wrong to suppose that this unwillingness to use her home language is indicative of a rejection of her home culture, or a sign that she is embarrassed about it. For she actively expresses her home culture in other ways, for example when choosing clothes in the home corner, making chapatis in the sandpit or seeking out dual-language books in Urdu and English.

Use of language

Although she can be at times fairly shy, and will allow her best friend to dominate group situations, Thaeba is generally confident in her use of English. She will readily initiate conversations with peers and, especially, adults. She talks for purely social reasons and also to get something she wants. In the latter instance she uses an appropriate register, for example when she asked me: 'Can you open my drink, please.'

She uses structured sentences with a fairly well developed vocabulary, although she is more interested in communicating meaning than in correctness, for example when talking excitedly about her birthday: 'Today it's my birthday in November.' However, such 'mistakes' are common in young native speakers as well as in young bilinguals. It is often difficult or impossible to tell whether Thaeba's non-standard usage of English – for example over-use of the indefinite article as in 'Look at a lollipop I'm making' – is due to her age or to her bilingualism.

She often uses chunks of correct English, particularly phrases used frequently by teachers. There are also strong traces of London English present in her speech, including 'gonna' (going to), 'hisself' (himself) and 'shame!' She can copy both English and Urdu, and does so in the right directions. She is familiar with books and stories, can find the first page and point to the text, moving her finger along it (though in both directions).

Keen to communicate meaning: Mohammed

Family

Mohammed is just six. He has an elder brother and sister, and there are also three children younger than himself in his family, two of them twins. He was born in Mogadishu, Somalia. He came to Britain a few months ago with his family from Somalia, after two years in a refugee camp in Kenya and a long journey through Yemen and Egypt. His father was a businessman, his mother a housewife. He lived in a large house with his paternal grandparents, his parents and his elder brother Ibtisan, his elder sister Aqmal and his younger twin brother and sister, Turnsil and Amina.

In 1993 the whole family left Somalia (Mohammed himself at the time was about three and a half), driven out by the civil war. They spent two years in a refugee camp in Kenya before embarking on a journey through Yemen and Egypt to Britain. They have been granted refugee status and now live in a small flat close to Mohammed's school.

Mohammed himself did not directly experience the war and was sheltered from its worst traumas. But it touched his larger family dramatically and caused a total dislocation to his whole life-world.

Mohammed has been at school in London for two terms. Despite the turmoil and trauma in his family's experience he has settled quickly and apparently easily. His family are involved with the local Somali community and all are practising Muslims. But he does not attend a community or mosque school, and his parents are not actively teaching him Arabic or Somali at home. He likes watching videos and is currently much into Power Rangers, which he also has as toys.

Repertoire

Mohammed has wide linguistic experiences. His parents speak Somali and some English but the main language at home is Arabic, and this is the first language which Mohammed learnt. He speaks to his parents in Arabic and also sometimes to his grandparents. With his brothers and sisters, however, he tends to use English and Somali. His family often make telephone calls to Somalia, as is customary in the Somali community in London, and Mohammed talks with his cousins during these calls in Somali.

School

At school Mohammed usually speaks English but is happy to use his other two languages as well. He recently offered spontaneously to act as an English-Somali interpreter for a newly arrived child in his class, and until then his class teacher was unaware that this was one of his skills. On another occasion he worked enthusiastically as a member of a group making a dual-language text in Somali and English on numbers and shapes. He could readily identify and name the shapes in both languages and played a leading role in organising the layout of the book and assigning tasks for the other children to perform.

Mohammed is very aware of the range of languages around him in the school. 'All friends I have,' he said the other day, 'one speak Urdu, one speak English, one speak Somalia [sic], one speak Arabic.' He rates himself as good at English and very good at Arabic but says he knows Somali 'just a little'. He says that he thinks in English.

Use of language

Mohammed is making striking progress as a user of English and is increasingly confident in initiating conversations with adults. He is more reserved with his peers but is taking an increasingly active role in activities. He is keen to communicate meaning in his speech and stories and as yet does not bother about accuracy. For example, he doesn't change verb forms according to whether the verb's subject is singular or plural ('she speak Arabic') or with regard to tense ('she push me'). Nor, often, does he distinguish between nouns and adjectives (Somalia/Somali, England/English). He frequently omits both definite and indefinite articles ('I can fly with airplane', 'I did first face, then neck'). He sometimes disorders the sequence of words in a sentence (as in the remark just cited, 'I did first face, then neck') and tends to use small chunks of learnt language as catch-all phrases, for example 'this one'.

Mohammed readily mimes words he doesn't know in English, for example 'over' and 'think', or borrows freely from his two home languages to supplement his English. He can describe objects in English in terms of size, shape and colour, and he makes contrasts by using modifiers such as 'very' and 'a little'. He talks about Somalia but generally his English is about concrete situations and tasks not abstractions.

Mohammed enjoys looking at books and is keen to share with an adult. He knows large chunks of Jill Murphy's *Whatever Next?* by heart and reproduces them with a high degree of memory, moving his finger from left to right on the page and claiming proudly that he is reading. He still pretends to read when he does not know the text, or even when there is no text, but produces a string of meaningless sounds approximating to English and spoken in a dull monotone, as if he has gathered that a dull monotone is the 'correct' way of reading aloud. The class teacher has done a lot of work on word recognition using flashcards. When tested, Mohammed showed that he knows 'see', 'and', 'a', 'I', 'can' and 'the'.

Juggling all the time: Usha and Lena

Usha and Lena are sisters, and were respectively aged 15 and 13 when this conversation with their teacher was recorded. The transcript has been edited slightly, to remove hesitations and repetitions, and also shortened. The teacher speaks first:

T   Can you tell me what memories you have of first learning English?

Usha   Okay, when we went to nursery school, our parents would talk to us in Gujerati, so ... when we went to nursery school the teachers found it very hard to communicate with us ... our English wasn't very good, but it was enough to communicate with the teachers ...

Lena   Mmm, there was mum and dad, they helped.

Usha   Yeah, they talked to us in English, or what they knew ... That's how it is with most Asian kids, I think.

Lena   Yeah, it didn't take us long, we were about three or four years old.

Usha   So we were learning English, we spoke English and then when we went to family functions or something like that, they were like: 'Don't you know Gujerati?' They found it really weird ... Then, when you're a bit older, you sort of mix, juggle the two languages together and you have a sort of English-and-Gujerati (*laughs*), you make your own language.

Lena   There was one point where we would speak Gujerati using a few English words (laughs) and vice versa. We'd speak Gujerati to our parents, especially to mum and then we'd say something in English in between. It didn't really bother our parents, 'cos they knew that we knew.

Usha   Yeah, like 'Pass the chair – the whole sentence would be in Gujerati, except, like, 'the chair', it'd be in English. And we'd always say 'please' as well, so that it became part of Gujerati as well.

T   So you switch, you juggle languages all the time. What's that like?

Lena   Well, it's quite fun in a way, isn't it?

Usha   Yeah, it's nice to be able to speak Gujerati, communicate with your family in the home and the outside world as well, speak to them in English.

Usha   Yeah, I started learning Gujerati reading and writing around when I was about eleven or twelve years old, and when I started learning it, it really helped me, it actually enhanced my talking skills, my speaking skills in Gujerati, so that helped me a lot.

T   Why do you think that was?

Usha   Well, my mother and father wanted me to learn Gujerati properly, without having to use English as well.

Lena   I didn't really want to take the subject, I actually wanted to do German, but I thought I should learn Gujerati, it's what I do every day with my parents, when I go to India. It was mum's idea, she said 'Look, you should take Gujerati'.

Usha   It's part of your culture – you should take it.

Lena   Yes, it's part of your culture.

'I won': Andreia

Life was never smooth for me when I was in Brazil. I used to be 'the Idiot' of the class with a capital I. All I ever wanted to do was to get out of school and go to live very, very far away. The reason for all this unhappiness was a thirteen year old boy (same age as me) that amused himself by humiliating me. Today I would give him a freezing look and say the most offensive thing that occurred to me at the moment, but at the time I was an unsure, insecure, really thin and spotty thirteen year old girl. In a slow, painful and irreversible process he hardened me inside. A lesson I will never forget, and that was really useful in what was to come.

At the time that she wrote this 'language autobiography' Andreia was 15 years old.

When my dad told us that we might be coming to England, better still to London, I thought, 'I will be free of him, of this school, I will make a new start!' I was really happy. I didn't take into account the language, the problems, anything. I was just so overjoyed I could escape that I forgot all about it, until it slapped me in the face on the first day at school. Of course I knew it would be hard and tough, but I still didn't know how much as we approached the school that warm morning in October.

The first thing that struck me when I was left alone with the English speakers was that I couldn't ask anything, I couldn't talk! Millions of questions formed themselves in my head, but the problem wasn't asking them, the problem was that the questions were in … Portuguese.

On the first day I felt like a new animal in the zoo, being surrounded by everybody, asking and speaking in funny sounds that made no sense to me, but with which they communicated between themselves. I felt strange, but welcomed. I thought they would teach me everything, would be patient, but time proved me wrong.

They were amused on the first day, but by the second day they were used to me, my 'babysitter' was tired of being it, and me, I was thrown around like some sort of funny animal that amused people for a time, but not for long. They got bored and I got isolated .. and people started to make my life hell.

First they would pick on me for any reason, pushed me, shouted, gave me the cold shoulder and wanted to pick fights with me for no reason whatsoever. They, with some exceptions, ignored me when I tried to make conversations and didn't want me in their groups. I was a frightened little rat thrown in a corner with no defence.

I cried, I cried a lot, but only for myself. Nobody would see it. I had to make my way through. At least I wasn't alone. There was somebody that helped me a lot. His name was Pablo and he was the Spanish assistant. Before I learned to speak English, I would go every Wednesday to spend lunchtime with him and talk a lot in a funny mixture of Spanish and Portuguese. It was soothing being with him and it also gave my ears a rest. The funny thing is that before I came to England I couldn't understand a word of Spanish. Desperation does wonders for you.

I learned to speak English reasonably fast. I think that what made me learn English so fast was my instinct of survival as well as desperation. I needed to survive in my new environment and to do that I needed to speak the language. In three months I spoke English roughly but I still had a long way to go.

Although I talked to Pablo I still felt afraid and lonely, horribly lonely. Though I didn't feel much inclined to get out of my shell because I was hurt and afraid of everybody. Loneliness is bitter and I was becoming more and more bitter.

One of my classmates said something that turned my bitterness into anxious expectation, she said, 'Give yourself time to learn, to be accepted as a member of our class. Rushing things won't help you.' So I waited and started being a friend of many people. As I waited I found out that I had been blamed for situations that happened before I came to England!

In the beginning, when I couldn't speak, I wished desperately that a group of Brazilian teenagers that lived with their parents at Swiss Cottage would call me, be my friends and everything, but they didn't appear to care about me.

Now, I know it was all worth it. It doesn't matter how much suffering I had, in the end I won. I have true friends, I speak good English (reasonably, anyway) and I am preparing myself to do the Cambridge Proficiency. I won this round of the fight. I won.

The End?

Becoming and being bilingual: some points arising

The case-studies of Thaeba, Mohammed, Usha, Lena and Andreia illustrate several important points about the acquisition of an additional language, and about the role and responsibilities of teachers. These are noted below under the headings of 'diversity and complexity', 'listening to children', 'self-awareness about language', 'connections', and 'routes for bilingual learners'.

Diversity and complexity

The term 'bilingual', when applied to Thaeba and to the others, clearly refers to a wide range of competence. It does not necessarily imply the ability to speak two or more languages with equal fluency in all situations and for all purposes. Such ability is in fact extremely rare, even amongst the most brilliant linguists and amongst professional interpreters and translators. Rather, the term is used to recall and stress that children learning English as an additional language have experiences, knowledge, resources and skills which should be valued and built on, not neglected or ignored. The all-too-common term 'EAL children' implies subliminally that such children have a weakness to overcome, and that there is a deficit to be made good. The much more positive term 'bilingual' reflects respect for strengths which children already have, and for the potential which they are developing.

Listening to children

The teacher who compiled the profiles of Thaeba and Mohammed derived considerable personal and professional benefits, as did the teacher who interviewed Usha and Lena and transcribed the conversation. Not all teachers, of course, have the time to compile detailed profiles of all the children they teach. All, however, can make a point of knowing as much as possible about the languages which their pupils speak, and of the varying contexts in which they speak them. Such awareness is an essential part of listening to children, both literally and metaphorically.

Self-awareness about language

The case-studies were valuable not only for the teachers but also for the children and young people. Their reflections on their own learning will stand them in excellent stead when – for example – they consider, consciously or intuitively, the differences between conversational English on the one hand and curriculum English on the other.

Connections

All the case-studies illustrate the point expressed in the diagram which appeared here earlier as Figure 1: development of an additional language goes hand-in-hand with cognitive development, academic development and personal development.

Routes for bilingual learners

The case-studies recall and illustrate the distinction which may be made between conversational English (sometimes known as BICS – Basic Interpersonal Communicative Skills) on the one hand and curriculum English (CALP – Cognitive Academic Linguistic Proficiency) on the other. (See, for example, *Negotiating Identities* by Jim Cummins, full details on page 71.) All the young people in the case-studies are clearly proficient, or quickly becoming proficient, in the English of everyday communication. What is essential, however, is that they should be proficient also in the English of the national curriculum. (Please note: the principal differences between everyday English and curriculum English are listed in Figure 5 on page 34.)

Theorists draw a distinction not only between everyday English and curriculum English but also between high and low levels of cognitive challenge. The two sets of distinctions can be used to create a simple matrix, as shown in Figure 2 overleaf, referring to four different types of language use. All four are important and valuable, for all children. For bilingual children it is particularly important that they should have plenty of opportunities to use what the matrix calls Type 3 language – interactive, but with high cognitive demands. Their route, so to speak, from Type 1 (everyday conversation) to Type 4 (curriculum language) has to involve spending quite a lot of time with Type 3. Much of this book is about how this route through Type 3 may be planned in practice.

Register of English	Level of cognitive challenge	
	Low	*High*
Everyday	Type 1: for example, chat about everyday events and plans, and about TV programmes, pop stars, sports, etc.	Type 3: for example, talk within the context of structured exercises and activites which require genuine communication.
Curriculum	Type 2: for example, giving rote-learned answers, copying from books, doing 'comprehension' exercises.	Type 4: for example, writing answers in SATs and GCSE and written work in preparation for all such tests.

Figure 2: Examples of four types of language use

Notes

This matrix is derived from the theoretical work over the years of Jim Cummins, of the Ontario Institute of Studies in Education – see for example his book *Negotiating Identities*, full details on page 71. Much of our own book is about practical ways of enabling children to use Type 3 language, in order that they may become proficient also in Type 4 language, i.e. the language which is essential for academic success.

Places to go, things to do: routes for bilingual learners

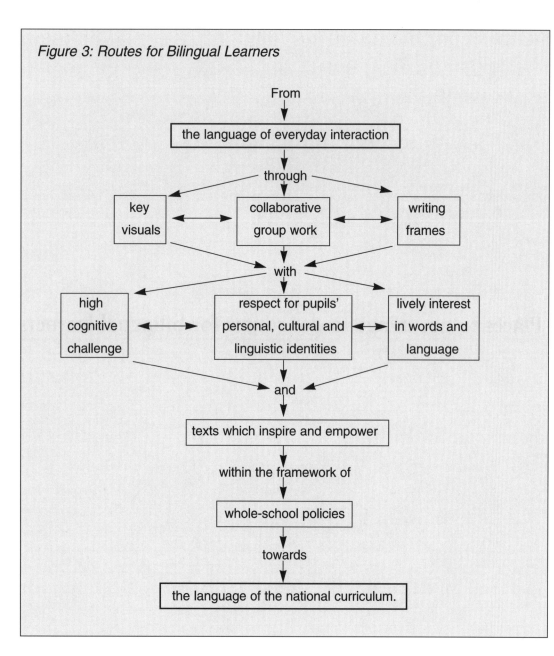

Figure 3: Routes for Bilingual Learners

From
↓
the language of everyday interaction
↓
through
↓
key visuals ←→ collaborative group work ←→ writing frames
↓
with
↓
high cognitive challenge ←→ respect for pupils' personal, cultural and linguistic identities ←→ lively interest in words and language
↓
and
↓
texts which inspire and empower
↓
within the framework of
↓
whole-school policies
↓
towards
↓
the language of the national curriculum.

Figure 3 stresses the key idea that the route for bilingual learners from everyday English to curriculum English needs to go via classroom activities which make much use of key visuals, collaborative groupwork and writing frames, and which involve high levels of cognitive challenge, a genuine respect for children's personal, cultural and linguistic identities, a lively interest in words and language, and the use of inspiring and empowering texts.

In the following pages we discuss and illustrate four of these points in greater detail: **key visuals** (pages 25-33), **collaborative groupwork** (pages 34-41), **writing frames** (pages 42-45), and **ways with words** (pages 46-48). We recall at one stage the nature of **cognitive challenge** (pages 40-41). In an earlier section of the book (pages 11-20), we discussed aspects of children's identities.

In a later section (pages 49-57), we discuss **inspiring and empowering texts.**

Key Visuals – *access through seeing*

What is a key visual?

In principle, any kind of pictorial material can act as a key visual. It is key if it illustrates, communicates, summarises or synthesises a key idea, notion or understanding. So examples of key visuals include:

- road signs – the internationally agreed symbols for children crossing, slippery road surface, loose chippings, deer jumping out at you, and so on

- signs at airports and in town centres, similarly international, trans-national and communicative, regardless of any language

- national flags

- icons on the computer screen

- religious art

- great news photographs

- great cartoons

- advertisements

- and, **particularly important in educational settings**, visual models such as matrices, grids, tabulations, pie-charts and histograms, decision trees and branching diagrams, mental maps and spider charts, flow charts, tick charts, time lines, Venn diagrams and topic webs. What makes these invaluable in educational settings is that they can literally be taken apart and then re-constructed, and can therefore communicate and develop understanding of complex relationships. In this book itself, Figure 1 (page 7) is an example of a Venn diagram, Figure 2 (page22) is an example of a 2 x 2 matrix, Figures 3 (page 24) and 4 (page 27) are examples of flow charts and Figure 5 (page 34) is an example of a tabulation. At inset sessions all these figures could valuably be built up piecemeal, and colleagues could be encouraged to design their own with the same subject-matter.

Context and purpose

The difference between a key visual and any other sort of illustration is that the former **expresses and communicates a key idea**, something really important. Whether or not an idea is important, and therefore key, depends on context, role and purpose – whether you're driving a car, or are a religious believer, or using your computer, or trying to find your way round an airport, or advertising a product, or wanting to buy something. Or, of course, whether you're teaching science or history, geography or PSHE. In educational settings, the most valuable types of key visual are those which can literally be taken apart and then re-assembled, bit by bit.

Though for fostering language development, *all* kinds of key visual are valuable. For all can be used to provide opportunities for the fundamental human activities of encoding, de-coding and translating. Fluent and agile switching backwards and forwards between iconic and linguistic forms of communication is analogous to switching ('juggling', to recall the word used by Usha and Lena on page 17) between two or more different languages, or between different registers or dialects within the same language. Fluency and agility within Standard English, particularly in writing, are essential ingredients for educational attainment.

Developing and using key visuals

Put abstractly, there are several separate but inter-related questions when you set about creating or selecting a key visual. These are presented in the form of a flow chart (a key visual) in Figure 4. As a series of simple bullet points, the questions are as follows:

- What is the 'big idea' – the key concept – we want children to learn?
- What visual material shall we choose or create to encode this key idea?
- How shall we present and use the visual material, bearing in mind (a) the need to activate and draw on children's existing knowledge, (b) the need to ensure that they learn and use specialist terms and (c) the desirability of using collaborative groupwork?
- What shall we do to enable children to consolidate and apply their new knowledge?
- How shall we review what happens, in order to improve our own teaching?

The chart which appears here as Figure 4 is developed from an idea in Steve Cooke's booklet *Collaborative Learning Activities in the Classroom*. The booklet has many fascinating examples of key visuals, and many excellent suggestions for using them. Full bibliographical details on page 71.

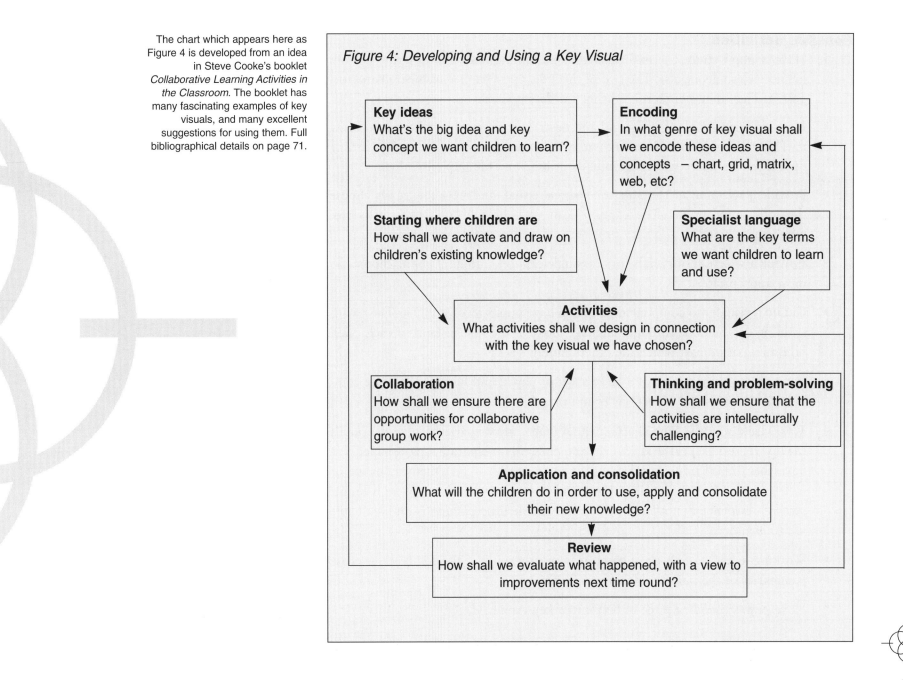

Figure 4: Developing and Using a Key Visual

Key ideas
What's the big idea and key concept we want children to learn?

Encoding
In what genre of key visual shall we encode these ideas and concepts – chart, grid, matrix, web, etc?

Starting where children are
How shall we activate and draw on children's existing knowledge?

Specialist language
What are the key terms we want children to learn and use?

Activities
What activities shall we design in connection with the key visual we have chosen?

Collaboration
How shall we ensure there are opportunities for collaborative group work?

Thinking and problem-solving
How shall we ensure that the activities are intellectually challenging?

Application and consolidation
What will the children do in order to use, apply and consolidate their new knowledge?

Review
How shall we evaluate what happened, with a view to improvements next time round?

Possible activities

- Have a pupil study a visual for (say) one minute and then describe it from memory to someone else. The two of them discuss what is remembered and forgotten. Then they switch roles, using a different visual.

- Have one pupil look at the visual and describe it to another, who has to draw it. This activity is sometimes known as a 'barrier activity' if it involves setting up a small screen between the pupil describing and the pupil listening.

- Provide a selection of captions for a single visual, and have the pupils choose the most appropriate. The captions can of course be oblique – proverbs, quotations, snatches of poetry or verse – as well as reasonably obvious.

- Provide a selection of visuals for one single caption, and have pupils choose the most appropriate.

- Cut up a visual into component parts and have pupils reconstitute it. The reconstituting can be done through language alone in the first instance if each pupil holds a separate part which the others cannot see.

- Put a visual in the centre of a large sheet of paper, and have pupils write comments, questions and reflections round the edges.

- With visual models, flow charts, mental maps, topic webs, etc, give the pupils the raw materials (i.e. the key words and phrases) on separate slips of paper, and have them build up a visualisation of their own – or give them guidance or instructions. Have them add colours and pictures or symbols – there is ample research evidence that adding colour and simple little pictures is an invaluable aid to memory.

- Working as individuals or in pairs or in small groups, have pupils write prose summaries of the points which a visual encodes.

- Have pupils encode a piece of text into a key visual.

Key visuals: an exploration of words

Key /*n.&* v. **1** an instrument for opening or locking. **2** what gives or precludes the opportunity for or access to something. **3** (*attrib*) essential; of vital importance (*the key element in the problem*). **4** a place that by its position gives control of a sea, territory etc. **5a** a solution or explanation. **5b** a word or system for solving a cipher or code. **6** a piece of wood or metal inserted between others to secure them. **7** the part of a first coat of wall plaster that passes between the laths and so secures the rest. **8** the roughness of a surface, helping the adhesion of plaster etc.

Cf **key industry**, an industry essential to the carrying on of others, e.g. coal-mining, dyeing. **key map**, a map in bare outline, to simplify the use of a full map. **keynote**, a prevailing tone or idea (*the keynote of the whole occasion*). **keystone**, the central principle of a system, policy, etc. on which the rest depends.

Synonyms: **n.** answer, clue, cue, explanation, guide, indicator, sign, solution, translation. **adj.** basic, chief, crucial, decisive, essential, fundamental, important, leading, main, major, pivotal, principal.

Visual /*adj. & n.* **adj.** of, concerned with, or used in, seeing. **-n.** a visual image or display, a picture.

Cf **vision n. 1** a thing or idea perceived vividly in the imagination (t*he romantic vision of youth; had visions of warm sandy beaches*). **2** imaginative insight. **3** statesmanlike foresight; sagacity in planning.

Cf **visualise** v.tr. make visible esp. to one's mind (a thing not visible to the eye). *Synonyms*: conceive of, conjure up a mental picture of, envisage, imagine, picture, see in the mind's eye.

Key visuals in multilingual classrooms

Key visuals are invaluable in all classrooms and all schools, but are particularly useful in multilingual settings. For they are relevant for the four main kinds of learning included in the diagram on page 7, relating respectively to pupils' academic development, cognitive development, language development and personal development:

Academic development

Key visuals can communicate essential ideas and concepts in national curriculum subjects, and can therefore promote knowledge and understanding independently of pupils' competence in English.

Cognitive development

Key visuals can develop generic cross-curricular skills, and work with them can be cognitively challenging and engaging independently of pupils' competence in English. For example, they can involve and stretch pupils in tasks of classifying, categorising, linking and organising; observing and memorising; sequencing in time and in causality; predicting, hypothesising and testing; and so on. Of course, it may often be valuable for bilingual children to discuss them in their first language as well as, or instead of, in English.

Language development

Key visuals can develop both oracy and literacy, for they foster spoken language and enable pupils to explain, justify and advocate more fully than they could with words alone. Also, they can be invaluable as preparatory for a writing task and for explaining a piece of text.

Social and personal development

Key visuals can be used in groupwork and pairwork to develop self-esteem and interpersonal and social skills.

Decision trees

The topic was **leaves** in Key Stage 2 Science. First, the children went on a nature walk in the cemetery behind the school, to collect different kinds of leaves. Each group was accompanied by a parent. Before leaving the classroom all children and parents were given an explanation, and in particular were instructed about how to tell the difference between a simple and a compound leaf. All children played a full part, including those still at the beginning stage of learning English. All seemed inspired and motivated by the strong visual and tactile stimuli.

Back in the classroom, the children sorted their leaves in as many different ways as possible – simple and compound, spiky-edged or not, hairy or not, and so on. Parents sat with the groups, and encouraged language of comparison and classification, using a language sheet which the teacher had provided for them. (Examples included: 'These leaves are similar because they ...' and 'These are different because ...' and various adjectives such as hairy, spiky, smooth.) They described their leaves as accurately as possible in conversation, and then drew them with written descriptions. They then used a tick chart entitled A Closer Look at Leaves to itemise the features which each leaf possessed (oval, saw-toothed, compound, pinnate, etc) and were required to use the technical terms orally in their talk with each other and with the parents.

In the next lesson, the teacher explained the idea of a decision tree. Ahmed and Rickesh, still at the earliest stages of learning English, were readily able to follow the tree with their fingers and to produce a list of written information about each leaf, for example:

It is a simple palmate leaf with smooth edges.

The top of the leaf and the bottom of the leaf are both smooth.

This leaf has a round shape with pointed ends.

It is a simple pinnate leaf.

This has a saw-toothed edge.

In later lessons, the teacher used pictures of animals in order to create and use decision trees, and also grids and matrices. This work, too, seemed to be successful in developing children's language, though clearly some children seemed to benefit less when working with pictures than from the tactile, three-dimensional and manipulative aspects of the activities with leaves. The teacher resolved to use models of animals another time, to see if this proved to be more engaging and motivating. Her overall view was that all the children (not only those who were bilingual) had definitely developed a greater command of specialist vocabulary than had the previous year's class.

Structure and Sequence – using story grids to explore and extend

Grandpa's Handkerchief

This book by Dorothy Clark is the story of Grandpa's week. On each day of the week he uses a different coloured handkerchief for a different purpose. First, the children became familiar with the story. They then showed their knowledge of the story's content, structure and sequence by completing a story grid.

Each pair or group had a copy of the chart enlarged to A3 size, and a set of 'answer slips'. Through discussion they agreed on where the slips should be placed, and then checked with the original text. After pasting or blutacking the slips in place, they used their grids to re-tell the story.

Next, they used their grids to develop the story, and to create different stories with the same or a similar repetitive structure. For example, they were encouraged to use a different set of sequencing markers, instead of the days of the week; to use more precise descriptions of colour and appearance; to think up different objects, in addition to the handkerchief; and to think up new uses for the handkerchief. Next, these new grids were used to tell the new stories, both orally and in writing.

Other possible stories

Any story with a strong repetitive pattern can lend itself to the construction of a sequence and structure grid. Examples include *Tortoise's Dream* by Joanna Troughton, *Squeak-a-Lot* and *Farmer Duck* by Martin Waddell, *The Shopping Basket* by John Burningham, *Eat Up Gemma* by Sarah Hayes, and *On the Way Home* by Jill Murphy.

Day of the week	Colour	Use
Monday	blue	to wipe away a crumb
Thursday	red	to make a sun hat
Wednesday	green	to cheer the team
Tuesday	pink	to remind him about a birthday
Sunday	orange	to play pirates
Saturday	white	to wave a train
Friday	yellow	to bandage a knee

Structure Charts – four sets of uses

Children learning English as an additional language need to develop (a) cognitively, (b) academically and (c) personally as well as (d) linguistically. In terms of this fourfold task, a structure chart such as the one shown for *Grandpa's Handkerchief* opposite has the following uses.

Academic

Grids based on stories involve all four aspects of English:

Reading: a grid helps develop skills of comprehension and prediction, awareness of left-right and top-down orientation, the building of a sight vocabulary, and of course an appropriate context for the teaching of phonics.

Listening: a grid helps children to listen to a story more actively than if they were provided with words, or words-and-pictures, alone.

Writing: a grid provides a structure for children to write their own stories, and is indeed a kind of writing frame. It shows conventions of starting; ways of describing problems, disorders and threats; reconciliations, resolutions and redress; and conclusions. It naturally requires proper use of paragraphs (each row) and sentences, clauses and phrases (each cell) and appropriate punctuation (particular cells require recurring markings). It may well introduce and stress the difference between spoken and written language.

Talking: a grid promotes speculative and reflective talk, and also explaining and justifying. Children may well have to engage in naming. ('What do all the pictures in the second column have in common?' asked a teacher compiling a chart for Jill Murphy's *On the Way Home* – 'They all show *scary* creatures,' came the reply.)

Cognitive

Working with a matrix is an archetypal activity of comparing and contrasting, and therefore of categorising and conceptualising. The recognition of similarities and differences, and that two phenomena can be similar in one respect but different in another, is at the heart of all learning, in all curriculum subjects.

A grid involves manual and tactile activity by pupils as well as verbal and pictorial activity, and is therefore likely to help them memorise better and to learn. Also it involves them in working with a whole pattern as well as with separate fragments, thus increasing their understanding. It may involve the use of both logic and imagination.

Linguistic

The text used in a story grid can be carefully chosen to rehearse specific grammatical structures – for example, prepositional phrases. Talk about the grid can involve much repeated use of key words such as What, Who, Why, Where.

The linguistic demands can readily be differentiated, such that all children, whatever their present competence, can be challenged to add to both their passive and active vocabulary.

Personal and cultural

Children can work with the grid in their home language as well as, or instead of, English. The story itself can draw on their personal and cultural experience, and that of their families and communities. Completing a grid can require genuinely collaborative groupwork, with real communicative tasks for each individual. A story about the resolution of problems and removal of threats to identity can help children cope with strong emotions. The activity of completing a grid is satisfying at quite a deep level, particularly if the story itself involves deep personal issues.

Figure 5 – Differences between everyday English and curriculum English

	Everyday English – for example, a conversation between two children the playground	Curriculum English – for example, a child writing in history, science or geography
Motivation for using language	To communicate, or to maintain a relationship with a peer	To demonstrate knowledge and understanding
Relationships with others	Very important	Less important
Sense of personal identity	Very important	Less important
Expression of personal feeling	Very common	Rare
Subject matter – (a)	Usually of immediate interest and relevance	Seldom of immediate relevance
Subject matter – (b)	Often about things which can be seen as the talk takes place	Seldom about things which can be seen as the writing takes place
Subject matter – (c)	Often about a shared experience	Seldom about a shared experience
Possibility of feedback	Immediate feedback given by others on how well one is communicating	Feedback not immediate, and may take hours or even days
Importance of non-verbal communication – tone of voice, facial expression, posture, gesture, body language, etc	Extremely important	Of no importance
Nouns	Mostly one or two syllables, derived from Germanic or Anglo-Saxon sources	Many of two or more syllables, and derived from Greek, Latin or French
Pronouns	Clear from situation what they refer to	Clarity depends on observing grammatical rules
Technical terms	Seldom used	Must be used
Register	Frequent use of slang and colloquialisms	Formal language essential
Importance of Standard English	Often not important, particularly if others present use non-standard vocabulary and forms.	Essential

Collaborative groupwork has two main features – (a) it involves a mix of everyday English and curriculum English, (b) it is cognitively challenging. It therefore provides an excellent context for children to meet, use and internalise academic terms and concepts. It is, in other words, an invaluable 'place to visit' on the journey from everday English to curriculum English. Other important places to visit are mentioned in the chart on page 24, 'Routes for Bilingual Learners'.

Collaborative Groupwork – the campaign for real communication

Introductory

One of the principal values of collaborative groupwork is that it provides opportunities for learning through talking – it helps children to move through and beyond everyday language into curriculum language. The tabulation opposite summarises the main differences between everyday English and curriculum English.

Other values include social skills, and the fact that sometimes – though not necessarily or always! – children learn more easily from each other than from a teacher. But for a range of reasons, exploratory and reflective talk can degenerate into mere chat, or can be dominated by one or two articulate or confident individuals. We recall here various simple ways of promoting talk rather than chat, and of ensuring that everyone is likely to take part.

The activities described on the following pages can be used with a wide range of curriculum subject-matter, and with children of all ages and levels of linguistic proficiency. It is sometimes useful to introduce and practise them with non-academic subject-matter in the first instance, before moving on to an aspect of the national curriculum.

When one is designing an activity it is useful to consider not only the academic knowledge and technical terms which are to be introduced and communicated but also the cognitive skills (as listed in this book on page 40, for example) which the activity will require.

1   One, two, four

Start by requiring each pupil to do or decide or write or choose something on their own. (If they write, provide a simple framework – a sentence-completion or writing-frame task, for example. And have them write in a box or on a slip of paper, not a large blank and maybe daunting sheet.) Then have them talk in pairs about what they have written or done. Then form fours or sixes. When pairs join others it can often be useful if individuals speak on behalf of their partners.

2   From listening to writing

This is a simple one, two, four activity which has great value in helping to develop proficiency in curriculum language.

First, the teacher reads at normal speed a short key text. It could be an entry in an encyclopaedia, a book review, a passage in a textbook, a newspaper article or editorial, an extract from a guidebook, and so on. The children listen without making notes. Second, the teacher reads the text again and this time children make notes of key words and phrases.

Third, children work in pairs, comparing their notes and adding to them.

Fourth, the children work in fours. Again they compare notes and add to them. The essential task now, however, is to re-constitute the original text as accurately as possible.

It will almost certainly then be valuable to compare the children's versions with the original, and to discuss the differences and similarities.

3   Objects to handle

Arrange for children to work with things which are tangible and which they can handle and arrange. Moving their hands seems to loosen their tongues and their minds. For example, provide phrases, statements and quotations on separate slips of paper, or (preferably) on cards. Also, of course, it is valuable to use three-dimensional objects. Specific tasks can include:

- sort the objects into pairs or into four (or whatever) categories, and use a dictionary or thesaurus to find a range of words which describe each category and differentiate it from others

- place the objects on a matrix or Venn diagram

- sequence the objects

- rank the objects according to specific criteria.

The Water Cycle

Working in groups of six, Year 3/4 children sequenced a series of statements about the water-cycle – these included 'clouds move towards land on onshore winds', 'streams join up to form rivers', 'high in the sky the air is cold', and 'water vapour rises in the warm air and causes clouds'. Such statements had also to be related to the three key concepts of evaporation, condensation and precipitation, and to some large illustrations. The children used mainly content cues to get the sequence right but were alert also to linguistic cues. They found the task engaging and enjoyable, and readily engaged in questioning, negotiating, arguing and justifying.

---

4   Precise tasks

This is a point relevant to all collaborative groupwork rather than an activity in itself. Always give precise unambiguous instructions about the actual outcome you want. 'Here are pictures of six people. Choose the two people you would most like to meet. For each of them write down the two questions you would most like to ask.' Tight and clear instructions, leading to an obvious outcome, are liberating rather than cramping. By the same token, vague instructions ('discuss what you think of this'), can merely dissipate energy and interest, and lead to much waste of time.

5   Brainstorming

This well-known activity is frequently invaluable. It involves the making of a list without any discussion in the first instance. If it goes well, everyone feels able and willing to contribute, existing knowledge is activated and pooled, and an atmosphere of openness and mutual trust is established. Further, the list which is generated can be a valuable basis for various ranking and sequencing activities. Of course, it is often valuable for bilingual children to brainstorm in their home language as well as in English.

6   Oral cloze

Another well-known activity, invaluable for introducing a new piece of material. Blank out or (if you are using a text in large print) place post-its over certain key words, or over every seventh word. When they have chosen a word to fill a gap, children can be required to consult a thesaurus to find a better word, or to reassure themselves that indeed the word they have chosen is the most appropriate. This develops sensitivity to nuances and gradations of meaning, and is a valuable stimulus to real discussion as different possibilities are compared and contrasted, and the final choice is made and justified.

7   Jigsaw exercises

Arrange for each pupil to have an essential piece of information which everyone else needs. Genuine collaboration is therefore necessary. Jigsaw exercises, for example: each pupil in the group has a fragment, written or visual, to contribute. The term jigsaw is also used to describe activities which involve pupils re-grouping, so that all members of a 'new' group know something which they learnt in an 'old' group, and which they now have to impart. (See 'Piecing the Pattern Together' overleaf for an example.)

8   Barrier games

Use a large book or sheet of cardboard to act as a barrier between two children, or between two pairs. They then have to engage in communication activities such as:

- A describes a picture and B has to draw it

- A describes an arrangement of objects and B has to re-create it

- A and B have slightly different versions of the same picture, and through discussion have to identify what the differences are

- A and B have identical maps, and give each other directions for moving from one place to another

- A and B each has a map or flow chart which is incomplete, and through discussion each has to complete the version which they have.

9 Kim's Game

This well-known activity can be valuably used to develop language if some of the objects are extremely similar to each other, so that careful observation and precise descriptions are required.

10 Re-constituting

Take two different texts and cut them up into their separate sentences, and shuffle all the fragments together. As a group, children have to sort the fragments into two clusters and then to sequence them. Or take ten (say) quotations, proverbs or sayings and cut each in half – again, the task is to re-constitute them. Such exercises can be made considerably more demanding if the fragments are dealt out as in a game of cards, with each child having their own 'hand' and being required to read their hand to others, rather than merely show it. This calls for careful listening, and much repetition.

11 Strip cartoons

Cut up a strip cartoon and give a section to each pupil. They describe their sections to each other, and decide what the best sequence would be.

12 Homing in

Give the group a large picture. It could be the representation of a scene, or could show lots of different dogs, say, or different cars, or different people. Each child in turn mentally selects an item, and the other members of the group have to home in on it by asking questions.

Piecing the Pattern Together – concepts, information and classroom

The topic was urban and rural life in a developing country, and was being studied as part of KS2 geography. Material from *Kenya is My Country* by Bernice and Cliff Moon was divided into four constituent parts, each part relating to a specific individual – their work, career, education, responsibilities, circumstances. The four individuals were Lucy, a student; David, a coffee farmer; Mildred, a bank manager; and Elphas, a schoolboy. The children were divided into groups, and each group became 'expert' about one of the individuals. The class was then re-grouped in order to fill in a summarising matrix for each of the four individuals. The exercise required genuine communication between children, and made strenuous cognitive demands. It was much enjoyed and led to much excellent writing.

	Occupation/ Study	Place of Work Study	Future Planning	General Information
Lucy				
David				
Mildred				
Elphas				

13 Dice and counters

Board games using dice and counters are valuable ways of introducing academic as well as (of course) non-academic subject-matter. They literally require turn-taking, and may therefore be valuable in encouraging turn-taking in the metaphorical sense also. When landing on a marked square, children are required to make a choice and to justify it to the other players, or else to provide a piece of information from a text.

14 Making and using key visuals

A group can be required to change a piece of text into a key visual – for example a flow chart, topic web or mind web – and then a different group can be required to 'translate' the visual back into a text.

15 Collaborative drafting

In the 'real' world of adults a great deal of real discussion (talk as distinct from chat) happens around the drafting and re-drafting of papers. Such discussion can readily be replicated in classrooms. In addition to drafting real texts from scratch, there are plenty of other possibilities as well – including the use of writing frames, cloze procedure, sequencing text which has been cut up, adding sentences or phrases in the best place, choosing between alternative phrasings to express the same idea, and so on.

The Labours of Heracles

The work on Heracles was part of a Year 3 topic on Ancient Greece. The children watched the Channel 4 video, and then were given a chart relating to the first three labours. There were three main questions for each labour: what was the task? how was it accomplished? what happened on Heracles' return? Children were given a collection of cards, many of which used the expressive language used in the video ('enraged', 'pinioned', 'concealed', and so on), and had to place them in the right places on the chart. At first they were daunted by the large number of cards (for there were several to sequence in each of the nine main cells of the 3 x 3 matrix). Nevertheless they were able to share out the tasks amongst themselves, and engaged in much negotiation, hypothesising and justifying. Their subsequent writing showed that they had remembered the storylines with great accuracy, and were able to use appropriately the unusual and challenging words to which they had been introduced.

Thinking and Reasoning – the nature of cognitive challenge

It is axiomatic throughout this book that the learning of English as an additional language should not be divorced from (a) cognitive development, (b) academic development and (c) personal and social development. What does the first of these terms, 'cognitive development', mean? What do EAL specialists and theorists mean when they insist that learning an additional language must contain elements of 'cognitive challenge'?

One approach to this question involves using the concept of 'thinking skills', and drawing rough-and-ready distinctions between five main clusters of activities. The activities overlap and interconnect, and cannot readily be presented in a tidy sequential list. However, a sequential list is better than nothing:

1   Comparing, contrasting and matching

2   Categorising, classifying and sequencing

3   Speculating, hypothesising, inferring and predicting

4   Evaluating and selecting

5   Explaining and justifying

In slightly more detail, and with reference to some of the distinctive language required by each, these five clusters of skills are summarised opposite.

Listed here are five main types of cognitive challenge. Corresponding to each kind of challenge, there are certain distinctive linguistic demands.

1 Comparing, contrasting and matching

The vast majority of human knowledge depends, in the first instance, on observing and investigating similarities and differences. 'This goes with this', 'that goes with that'. The distinctive language includes concrete nouns, everyday adjectives, adverbs of comparison, and possessives. Key words and phrases include *like, similar, same, different, features in common.*

2 Categorising, classifying and sequencing

Out of activities of comparing, contrasting and matching there develops the process of categorising and classifying – phenomena are clustered, on the basis of their similarities and differences, into discrete groupings. If the phenomena are events, their classification will almost certainly involve sequencing. The distinctive language includes generic nouns, references to amounts and scale, and connectives and prepositions of time. Key words and phrases include *characteristics, criteria, belonging, arrange, sort.*

3 Speculating, hypothesising, inferring and predicting

Having placed phenomena into categories, human beings make conjectures and generalisations about the underlying patterns and reasons. The distinctive language includes terms and tenses expressing conditions. Key words and phrases include *why?, can we explain? what might be the cause? what would happen if? what would be the result if?*

4 Evaluating and selecting

Choices have to be made between alternative and perhaps competing explanations. The distinctive language may include adjectives for describing emotions. Key words and phrases include *good idea, agree, disagree, prefer, appropriate, fair, important, urgent, priority.*

5 Explaining and justifying

The chosen explanations are justified with evidence, and with reference to generalisations, principles and rules. Potential objections are refuted. The distinctive language includes terms of cause and effect. Key words and phrases include *because, it follows, therefore, nevertheless, although, however.*

Frames and Frameworks – *skeletons and scaffolds to help children write*

Introduction

Teachers and theorists working with bilingual pupils frequently make a rough and ready distinction between 'stages one and two' on the one hand and 'stages three and four' on the other; or between basic inter-personal communicative skills ('BICS') and cognitive, academic and linguistic proficiency ('CALP'). It is widely agreed that more attention needs to be paid to stages three and four and to CALP; that this means focusing on writing skills; and that in particular teachers need to consider competence in non-fictional, non-narrative forms of writing.

To focus on writing in general, and non-narrative or non-chronological writing in particular, is by no means to deny the crucial importance of oracy or of stories. Rather, it is to stress that oracy and narrative do not automatically help children to develop the literacy skills which they need for academic success.

For many years teachers have used 'writing frames', though not always with that term, to help pupils write. They provide the bare bones, the skeleton, on which pupils put the flesh; or the branch structure of a tree on which pupils put the leaves and fruit; or the scaffolding within or next to which pupils erect a building. The third of these metaphors nicely captures the notion that the aim is to help pupils make freestanding buildings of their own. Scaffolding is a mere aid, and is one day removed and forgotten.

Continuing the metaphors from the construction industry, it is relevant to recall not only 'scaffolding' but also 'building blocks'. Instead of providing a framework, or in addition to providing it, teachers may provide the various basic materials. For example, various facts and ideas to be organised into an appropriate overall shape.

The most usual kind of writing frame is one which provides, as building blocks, the opening words for each of, say, six paragraphs.

Non-fiction genres – the Exeter project

A recent project on writing frames based at the University of Exeter, led by Maureen Lewis and David Wray, adopted a typology of non-fiction genres developed by linguistics theorists. According to this typology there are six main genres. Any one piece of extended writing can contain more than one genre, and usually does. But as a whole, a piece of writing is likely to belong to a single genre, according to its overall purpose. The six genres are:

1 Recounting

Describing an event or sequence of events in order to record, inform or entertain. It is a narrative genre, but not fictional. Usually uses past tense. Very frequently used in schools. Basic structure is typically threefold: (a) scene-setting, (b) account of events one at a time, (c) concluding reflection or judgement. Verbs mainly of acting and feeling. Emotive vocabulary and expressive adjectives. Connectives which show sequence in time: *later, meanwhile, after a while, in due course*. Writing frames fostering this genre can usefully require pupils to state what they learnt as well as what they did.

The University of Exeter project on writing frames is vividly described, with many excellent and thought-provoking examples, in two valuable publications by Maureen Lewis and David Wray, available from the Reading and Language Information Centre at the University of Reading. Full bibliographical details are on page 71.

2 Reporting

Describing a situation or set of phenomena, as distinct from events. Usually uses present tense. May of course include recounting (genre 1) embedded within it. Basic structure usually involves a description of separate parts or aspects of the whole. It may valuably require pupils to compare and contrast, and to use subject-specific and unemotive vocabulary. Key visuals such as grids, tabulations and matrices can be used as preliminary 'graphic organisers', in order to summarise points of contrast and comparison, before the writing itself begins.

3 Explaining

Describing how something works or operates, or why something happened. Typically uses present tense in science and the social sciences (including geography), but past tense in history. Similar to the reporting genre, and may well use pieces of reporting within it, but needs to be more tightly sequenced and logical, with one part leading naturally to another through a thread of cause and effect. Can include a range of explanations for a single situation or phenomenon, in which case the genre is moving towards discussion (genre 6).

4 Instructing

Describing a sequence of operations, for example giving instructions on how something is to be done. Examples include recipes, rules of games and travel directions. May use imperatives, or else the present tense. Structure often requires a statement at start of the overall purpose, and of materials, equipment or apparatus which are needed. Often accompanied by pictures, diagrams or maps, and often subject-specific vocabulary is necessary or appropriate. The separate parts typically need to be carefully sequenced – 'First, you... Then, you...'

5 Advocating

Outlining and promoting a point of view, opinion or argument. May well include recounting, reports and explanations (genres 1, 2 and 3) within it; may illustrate its conclusions with instructions (genre 4); and may contain an element of discussion (i.e. referring to a range of views – genre 6). But the essential purpose is to advocate a particular outlook. Basic structure usually involves a series of arguments, each supported by evidence or illustration. Much use of connectives such as *however, nevertheless, for example, on the other hand*. Opening sentence should ideally be arresting and immediately engaging. The concluding sentence is often a punchline. One traditional structure (as also in discussion) is thesis, antithesis, synthesis.

6 Discussing

Describing a range of viewpoints and ideas, with sufficient information and respect for diversity to enable the readers to make a judgement of their own. May contain recommendations and conclusions, but the writing is in the 'discussing' genre rather than 'advocating' if these are separate from the main body. Dividing line is blurred, however, since much advocacy masquerades as discussion. As with the advocacy genre, the basic structure usually involves a series of arguments, each supported by evidence or example, often within the overall framework of thesis, antithesis, synthesis. The opening sentence should ideally be arresting and immediately engaging. The concluding sentence may well recall and revisit how the writing began.

Points about classroom use

1 Four-stage process

A writing frame should be used only as one stage, the third stage, in a four-stage piece of teaching:

- **First**, an oral stage, involving demonstration, explanation and modelling by the teacher.

- **Second**, joint activity by teacher and pupils, as they complete a frame together.

- **Third**, the writing frame is used by pupils individually or in pairs or small groups.

- **Fourth**, independent writing. The fourth stage is, of course, the goal: at this stage the pupil has outgrown the frame, and the features of the genre have entered the pupil's own personal repertoire.

A transition phase between stages three and four involves pupils adding to and deleting from the frame with which they have been provided. Further, this transition phase may well involve their creating their own frame, tailored to the particular topic about which they are writing.

2 Big versions

It's useful to provide frames in large-scale versions; to add deletions, alternatives and corrections in order to emphasise that a frame is never more than a draft; to add pictures or drawings in order to stress metaphors such as branch, skeleton, web or scaffolding.

3 Help cards

It's useful also to provide frames in the form of help cards, which pupils can consult when they feel blocked.

4 Purposes

Writing frames should be fully integrated with specific curriculum content, not taught on their own. This means among other things that pupils should have a purpose for writing over and above the need to develop skill in a particular genre.

5 Levels of ability

Writing frames can be effectively used with pupils of all abilities throughout all key stages. Many teachers would say that they have their uses also in sixth forms, and in further and higher education.

6 Models of real writing

Pupils should have plenty of access to good non-fictional writing in all genres – particularly genres involving argumentation, discussion and persuasion, for example leading articles in a range of different newspapers.

7 Oracy in all genres

It is invaluable to construct situations which require pupils to use the genres orally as well as in writing. They frequently, of course, use the recount genre orally, in their interactions with each other and with their families. But they probably have few opportunities for extended oral use of the other genres unless this is consciously required by the teacher, and by the activities which the teacher designs.

An example of a writing frame in the advocacy genre, for completion by teachers at an inset session.

WRITING FRAMES

How can teachers help their pupils write fluently in the various styles and genres required by the National Curriculum? One way is through the use of writing frames. I wish to argue here that we should use writing frames more than we do. I have three main points to make.

First,...

Second,...

Third,...

There are, admittedly, dangers. For example,...

A further possible problem is that...

Such dangers can be avoided if...

All things considered, it is clear that...

Ways with Words – meanings, nuances and power

Most bilingual children readily acquire the everyday language of the playground and face-to-face interaction. Direct teaching of English vocabulary (as distinct from the provision of structured opportunities to practise English) is by and large not necessary. But if bilingual children are to develop proficiency in curriculum language they will benefit enormously from focused and explicit attention to a wider range of words and phrases than those which are required for everyday interaction. They need also, it follows, to be encouraged to take a lively interest in words – for example, metaphors, synonyms and antonyms, proverbs and sayings, and nuances and gradations of meaning. Further, they need to be keen, entirely consciously, to add to both their passive and active vocabulary.

We recall here some of the many different kinds of activity or exercise which teachers can use to extend and enrich their pupils' vocabulary, and to motivate and support them in their enquiries. The activities and exercises can be organised as one-off events, unrelated to any specific curriculum content. Also, they can of course be closely integrated with teaching and learning about a specific national curriculum topic. The origins and nuances of words and of their close synonyms can readily be mentioned incidentally in the natural course of classroom teaching.

For extended discussion and explanation of the theoretical basis for teaching directly about words and their meanings, and for a wealth of suggestions for practical and enjoyable activities, it is valuable to consult *What's In A Word?* by Norah McWilliam. The full bibliographical reference is on page 71.

Exploring meanings and nuances

Give the children a collection of objects. Have them choose an adjective to describe each from their existing knowledge. Then have them search through a thesaurus for synonyms, and choose the best word for each object. In their selection of the best word they may well wish to consider its derivation, and other words connected with it. It is also valuable if children are encouraged to coin new words, and to discuss, select and justify the best coinings. Bilingual children can of course be encouraged to consider synonyms in their home language.

Sources of metaphors and sayings

Give the children a collection of metaphors and sayings, and have them sort these according to the cultural or occupational contexts in which they first originated. Common contexts include agriculture, seafaring and domestic work in the past, and engineering, computing and sport in the present. Or give children a page from today's newspaper and have them find (say) ten metaphors. Then again, sort these according to the original situation from which they were transferred. Enquire, using bilingual dictionaries as well as children's own knowledge, and the knowledge of their parents and of colleagues who are bilingual, into equivalent or similar metaphors in other languages. For traditional English metaphors, consult books such as *Over the Moon* and *Make Hay While the Sun Shines*, both by Shirley Hughes and published by Faber.

Over the Moon

'I laughed aloud at the enthusiastic woman trying to tempt her stonily unresponsive grandmother to suck eggs. The illustration on the facing page is equally amusing. In 'tied to his mother's apron strings', the man in question is a casualty: thin, pinched, resigned and wearing checked carpet slippers. His mother is, clearly, a martinet. But at least he is still alive, unlike the dodo who ends the book with such wit...'

From a review by Kate Kellaway of *Over the Moon: a book of sayings* by Shirley Hughes, *The Observer*, 9 August 1998.

Origins and suggestions of words and phrases

On an earlier page (page 29) we copied selectively some explanations, definitions and synonyms from a dictionary and from a thesaurus in order to explore and explain the term 'key visual'. Such an activity can also be valuably done with children, to fill out a word's meaning, echoes and nuances. Further, words with the same or similar sounds can be added, and also words with similar meanings and antonyms. The keyword being explored should ideally, of course, be from a specific curriculum area, or may be a word such as 'metaphor' which is fundamental in the consideration and discussion of language. As with all work directly concerned with the meanings of words, it is valuable to draw on children's knowledge of equivalent words and phrases in other languages.

Puns and riddles

All children enjoy puns and riddles. The sense of humour reflected in such material may be exasperating or unfunny for the teachers. There is nevertheless a rich storehouse here for exploration. It is important that children should attend consciously to words which have the same or similar sounds but different meanings, and to the ambiguities which can therefore arise. Many of the activities listed earlier for collaborative groupwork (pages 35-39) can use puns, riddles and jokes as their basic material. Also real or imaginary howlers provide useful material.

Word of the week

Each week choose an unusual but interesting word for exploration. Where does it come from? What do its constituent parts mean or suggest? Who uses it, when and how? What is the equivalent word in certain other languages? Can all or most children make a point of using it, both orally and in writing, in the course of the week? At the end of term, can children remember the meanings of all the words which have been introduced?

Le Mot Juste

Year 5/6 children worked with the story *The Three Wolves and the Big Bad Pig*. They were given collections of adjectives – 'hostile', 'sensitive', 'generous', 'fearsome', 'fearful', 'belligerent', 'affectionate', and so on – and collections of verbs, including 'strutting', 'swaggering', 'counselling', 'prancing' and 'frolicking', and had to place these on a chart opposite the names of the various characters. Drawing partly on their existing knowledge but partly also on dictionaries and a thesaurus, they had to choose the best word in each instance and to justify it.

Transcribing

Have the children transcribe a piece of their own discussion, or – for example – an excerpt from a radio phone-in programme. It is valuable if they make two versions: (a) exactly what is said, including pauses, hesitations and self-corrections and all, and (b) a tidied-up version using the conventions of written English. Have them list the ways in which spoken and written English, in this particular sample, are different from each other.

Spotting errors

Give children a collection of errors of English usage, including mixed metaphors and ambiguities as well as mis-spellings, typographical errors and errors of grammar. Also include errors of appropriacy. Have the children correct the errors, but also analyse and sort them.

Headlines and slogans

Many newspaper headlines and advertising slogans use puns, or assume knowledge of well-known sayings. Make a collection of such material, and have children explain the various items.

Language Play

In a brief review of *Language Play* by David Crystal, a sub-editor on the *Guardian* writes: 'David Crystal delights in ludic linguistics but doesn't dismiss language play as mere entertainment, even as he gives us hundreds of amusing examples. He argues that such games are central to human communication – one rather undervalued in schools – and may even have been a spur to evolution. Pun my word, I always knew we sub-editors had a point in life.' (*Desmond Christy, 22 August 1998.*)

What's in a Word?

In her book *What's in a Word?*, Norah McWilliam provides many practical and inspiring ideas for exploring words and their meanings with bilingual learners. In this connection she stresses the importance of having appropriate dictionaries and thesauri always available. 'The important thing to convey to children,' she writes, 'is that dictionaries are powerful tools-of-trade in language acquisition.' She writes too that 'a school's book collection must include bilingual dictionaries for each home language spoken, and these must not be left to gather dust in the staffroom!' She recommends *Language Activator* and *Dictionary of Contemporary English* published by Longman, *Ringbinder Thesaurus* published by Collins, and *Children's Thesaurus* and *Children's Dictionary* published by Oxford University Press. Also valuable is the *Cambridge Picture Dictionary* (Cambridge University Press) by David Vale and Stephen Mullaney, and its connected project book. The publication details of *What's in a Word?* are in the bibliography on page 71.

Gradations

Give children six or so different ways of saying much the same thing – for example, six ways of saying thank you or sorry, or six ways of requesting, advising, enquiring or threatening. Have them grade these in terms of force or formality, and match them to situations where they would be most and least appropriate. Or give them six near synonyms from a thesaurus, and have them grade or rank these on a scale.

Tales and texts to inspire and empower

Tales and texts to inspire and empower

Introductory note

Becoming literate in English naturally includes encounter with texts. All primary classrooms contain texts which are stories. Not all stories, however, are equally appropriate for, and accessible to, bilingual children. We therefore itemise here some of the main questions which, we believe, should be asked about the stories which schools already have, and which should be asked whenever new purchases are being considered. In particular we hope these questions will be useful when schools review their stocks of fiction and poetry in the context of the National Literacy Strategy.

We illustrate our questions and criteria by referring to a number of books which we ourselves know and like. Our awareness in this connection is inevitably incomplete, however. There are many valuable books which do not happen to be mentioned here. Please note that we have only included books which are currently, so far as we know, still in print, and that we have made a point of mentioning books first published within the last five years, and/or available in dual-language forms or published by specialist publishing houses. Virtually all the books are fully illustrated, and can therefore be used with a wide age-range – few if any are so advanced in their text that they could not be used at Key Stage One and none are so elementary that they could not be used at Key Stage Two.

Enriching the Literacy Hour

All books mentioned here can be used as sources of enlarged key texts in the Literacy Hour. Also all can be used within other segments of the hour. Further, all can be explored and enjoyed outside the hour, and can be used in connection with other national curriculum subjects, including in particular art, history, music and science.

A Universal themes in the subject-matter

Do we have books which engage children by referring, explicitly or symbolically, to universal themes? If so, children are more likely (a) to feel reflected and included and (b) to be keen to know what happens. Also, they are more likely to be keen to return to the story and the teacher will be more able to use the story as a point of reference in discussions and conversations.

In the questions below, six major themes of universal importance are recalled

- identity and diversity
- family and relationships
- living in society
- the environment
- origins and purpose
- dreams and imagination

1   Identity and diversity

Do we have books which engage children by referring to issues of ethnic, cultural and linguistic identity, and relationships between ethnic groups?

Examples of books on universal themes of identity and relationships include *Tortoise's Dream*, *Something on my Mind*, *Maybe It's a Tiger*, *The Fire Children*, *All the Colours of the Earth*, *The Shepherd Boy*, *Beware Beware*, *Many Rivers to Cross*, *Amazing Grace*.

2   Family and relationships

Do we have books which engage children by depicting relationships in families and between friends, and referring to tensions and struggles as well as to pleasures and fulfilment?

Examples of books on universal themes of family and relationships include *Finished Being Four, I Don't Eat Toothpaste Anymore, Savitri, The Patchwork Quilt, Amaz and the Lion, Jamaica and Brianna, A Lullaby for Daddy, Hue Boy, Peace at Last, Little Tiger Get Well Soon, Time to Get Up, Moving, A Balloon for Grandad, The Big Big Sea, Mithu the Parrot, In a Minute, Songolo, You and Me Little Bear, Ganging Up, So Much, Lima's Hot Chilli, A Baby Just Like Me, Say It Again Grandma, Where's Gran?*

3   Living in society

Do we have books which engage children by depicting relationships between individuals and society, and which touch on struggles for justice?

Examples of books on living in society include *The Boy Who Sailed with Columbus, Rose Blanche, Nobody Owns The Sky, Mithu the Parrot, Blodin the Beast, I Want to Be an Angel, Jamaica's Find, Mufaro's Beautiful Daughters, The Whispering Cloth, Talking Walls, Amazing Grace, The People Who Hugged the Trees.* Non-fiction books include *Mandela, Time To Be Free.*

4   The environment

Do we have books which engage children by referring to relationships between human beings and nature, and which raise questions about conservation and care?

Examples of books on environmental issues include *The People Who Hugged the Trees, Oi Get Off Our Train, Whale Boy, The Seashell Song, The Night the Animals Fought, The Hunter, Arion and the Dolphin, Mother Eagle Brother Sky, Yohance and the Dinosaurs, The Cherry Tree, Kofi and the Butterflies, Jessica ...*

5   Origins and purpose

Do we have books which engage children by containing mythical or legendary explanations for puzzles and mysteries, for example the origins of the universe and life, the origins of certain customs, the origins of natural phenomena?

Good examples of books on universal themes of creation and origins include *The Fire Children, Turtle and the Island, Cactus and Eagle, Mother Eagle Brother Sky, A Promise to the Sun, The Village of Round and Square Houses, Bringing the Rain to Kapiti Plain ...*

Books which re-tell myths of heroes and heroines include *Rama and the Demon King* and *Savitri.*

6   Dreams and imagination

Do we have books which engage children by depicting dreams, visions and imaginings – of fulfilment and achievement, and of harmony and fairness?

Examples of books on universal themes of dreams and imagination include *Kim's Magic Tree, Boots for a Bridesmaid, Moonlight Sunlight, Tortoise's Dream, Toyin Fay, Yohance and the Dinosaurs, Send for Sohail, Babu's Day, The Snowy Day, Rata Pata Scata Fata, Dreamstealer, Nobody Owns the Sky, Tar Beach, The Hunter, The Girl Who Hated Books, The Whales' Song, The Seashell Song, The Garden, Toppicualo, Finish the Story Dad, A Dark Dark Tale, On the Way Home, Oi Get Off Our Train, Dave and the Tooth Fairy* ...

B   Characters and cultural milieu

Do we have books which engage children by reflecting, in their settings and characters, the everyday world which they themselves know?

If so, as with books on universal human themes, children are more likely (a) to feel reflected and included, as distinct from invisible, and (b) to be keen to know what happens. Also, they are more likely to be keen to return to the story. Further, the teacher will be more able to use the story as a point of reference in discussions and conversations. The notes below refer to five key points regarding characters and contexts: multi-ethnic society; the wider world; symbolic human beings; challenging stereotypes; shared heritage and frames of reference.

7   Multi-ethnic society

Do we have books which engage children by reflecting everyday life in modern multi-ethnic Britain, with a range of cultural and ethnic identities, and with (increasingly) people of dual heritage and a mix of cultural loyalties and belongings?

Examples of books with multi-ethnic settings include *Maybe It's a Tiger, An Angel Just Like Me, Send for Sohail, I Din Do Nuttin, The Balloon Detectives, Fire at Nelson Heights, Jamaica and Brianna, Tar Beach, Amazing Grace, A Baby Just Like Me, A Gift for Gita, The Girl Who Hated Books, Roses for Gita, In a Minute, Many Rivers to Cross, Jamaica's Find, A Present for Paul, Forest Whispers, Lights for Gita, Nobody Owns the Sky, Samira's Surprise, Samira's Eid.*

TALES AND TEXTS TO INSPIRE AND EMPOWER

8   The wider world

Do we have books which tell stories from other countries, particularly from outside Europe, and from the past as well as the present?

Good examples of books with a cultural milieu outside Europe include *Something on my Mind, A Balloon for Grandad, The Radish Thief, The Hunter, The Cherry Tree, The Calypso Alphabet, Mother Eagle Brother Sky, The Village of Round and Square Houses, Savitri, The Moving Mango Tree, Mufaro's Beautiful Daughters, Hue Boy, Say It Again Grandma, Mithu the Parrot, Yohance and the Dinosaurs, Faith Ringgold, Talking Walls, The Garden, Kofi and the Butterflies, Can I Buy a Slice of Sky?, Handa's Surprise, The Whispering Cloth, Babu's Day, The People Who Hugged the Trees, Turtle and the Island.*

9   Symbolic human beings

Do we have books which engage children by depicting human beings symbolically as animals? Other things being equal, such stories are more inclusive than those where the characters belong to a specific social and cultural setting.

Good examples of books with a cultural milieu involving animals rather than humans include *Tortoise's Dream, Squeak-a-Lot, Little Tiger Get Well Soon, Guess How Much I Love You, The Bad-Tempered Ladybird, Golden Bear, Moving, Farmer Duck, Elmer, Mr Archimedes' Bath, Mithu the Parrot ...*

10   Challenging stereotypes

Do we have books which engage children by challenging negative stereotypes about, for example, gender roles, or the elderly, or about people with disabilities?

Good examples of books which challenge stereotypes include *Boots for a Bridesmaid, ABC I Can Be, Mum Can Fix It, Amazing Grace, Ben Makes a Cake, The Frog Princess?, Princess Smartypants, Nobody Owns the Sky, Faith Ringgold, The Turbulent term of Tyke Tyler, Mary Cassatt, Tar Beach, Jamaica and Brianna, Grandpa Chatterji, Kick-off...*

11   Shared heritage and frames of reference

Do we have books which engage children by familiarising them with stories, legends, rhymes, proverbs, sayings, stock characters, hero and heroine figures, and so on, which belong to the shared cultural reference points in (a) their own community, (b) other communities with which they come in contact and (c) British society as a whole at this time in social and cultural history?

Good examples of books which refer to a shared heritage in Britain as a whole, and in some instances re-interpreting it, include *Each Peach Pear Plum, Peepo!, The Frog Princess?, Noah's Ark, Dem Bones ...* Anansi stories provide good examples of Caribbean traditions and heritage ... Examples from South Asia include *Rama and the Demon King*, and *Savitri. Over the Moon* and *Make Hay While the Sun Shines* are valuable introductions to traditional sayings and proverbs ... Aesop is well introduced by *The Very Best of Aesop's Fables.*

C Richness and quality of language

Do we have books which engage children by introducing them to key language patterns which they need in order to explore and communicate their own ideas, both orally and in writing?

If so, children are more likely to develop their linguistic repertoire, thus enhancing not only their literacy skills but also their understanding and learning in all parts of the curriculum. The notes below refer to three main points relating to language: repeated episodes and patterns; resonance and richness; and the role of illustrations.

12 Repeated episodes and patterns

Do we have books which engage children by containing a series of similar events and therefore repeated language patterns? Such books give the pleasure which comes from security and being able to predict some of what will happen, and help children to learn substantial chunks of useful language. They also lend themselves readily to dramatisation, both with live actors and in puppet plays.

Good examples of books which contain repeated episodes and language patterns include *Tortoise's Dream, Squeak-a-Lot, Farmer Duck, Grandpa's Handkerchief, The Shopping Basket, Eat Up Gemma, The Old Woman and the Pumpkin, On the Way Home, Oi Get Off Our Train, You and Me Little Bear, Where's Gran, Lima's Hot Chilli.*

13 Resonance and richness

Do we have books which engage children by containing language which is resonant and powerful as distinct from flat, and which uses alliteration and assonance, unusual and expressive words, puns, playfulness with language, the coining of new words, and metaphor and simile?

Good examples of books which contain rich and resonant language include *Moving, A Balloon for Grandad, Beware Beware, The Tree in the Wood, The Seashell Song, All the Colours of the Earth, Yohance and the Dinosaurs, Kofi and the Butterflies, The People Who Hugged the Trees* ...

And many poetry books, including *Tasty Poems, An Orange Poetry Paintbox, Say It Again Grandma, I Din Do Nuttin, Can I Buy a Slice of Sky?, Boing! Boing! Squeak, Splishes and Sploshes, Playtime Poems, Something Rich and Strange, Another Very First Poetry Book, Bibbilibonty, There's An Awful Lot of Wierdos in our Neighbourhood, Hairy Tales and Nursery Crimes, Not a Copper Penny in Me House.*

14 Illustrations

Do illustrations add to the story such that, for example, the text on its own is insufficient? Do they provide lots of talking points? Do they assist with understanding of key points in the story, and therefore with understanding of the text?

Virtually all the books listed on these pages have evocative and enjoyable illustrations. *Zoom* and *Window* are dependent on pictures alone. *Handa's Surprise* and *Who Sank the Boat?* are two of many where the text on its own is deliberately insufficient, and *Mr Archimedes' Bath* one of many where enjoyment comes more from the pictures than from the text itself.

D   Ambiguity, humour and links

15   Multi-layered meanings

Do we have books which engage children by containing a range of meanings and interpretations, such that for example they have significance for adults as well as children, and will yield additional meanings over time? If so, children are more likely to return to the book and their parents are more likely to enjoy sharing it with them.

Good examples of books with multi-layered meanings include *Tortoise's Dream, Maybe It's a Tiger, Beware Beware, The Girl Who Hated Books, All the Colours of the Earth, The Tree in the Wood, The People Who Hugged the Trees ...*

16   Humour

Do we have books which engage children by appealing to their sense of fun and humour?

Good examples of books enjoyable for their humour include *Maybe It's a Tiger, Squeak-a-Lot, Look Out Patrick!, On Friday Something Funny Happened, Who Sank the Boat?, The Frog Princess?, Farmer Duck, Over the Moon, Make Hay While the Sun Shines, Handa's Surprise, Mr Archimedes' Bath, Elmer, It Came From Outer Space, Jeremiah in the Dark Woods, The Radish Thief, Tasty Poems, Michael, The Very Hungry Caterpillar, Zoom ...*

16   Links with National Curriculum subjects and topics

Do we have books which engage children by familiarising them with concepts in non-fiction subjects and topics, for example in science, maths and history.

Examples include *Mr Archimedes' Bath, The Very Hungry Caterpillar, The People Who Hugged the Trees, Five Things to Find, Just a Pile of Rice, Who Sank the Boat?, Welcome Back Sun, Abena and the Rock, The Snowball Rent ...*

17   Availability in a range of formats and languages

Is a dual-language version of the story available? If so, in what other languages besides English? Is a tape-recording available? Or video? Is the story available in large format? Is there a poster? A jigsaw? Sequencing cards? CD Rom?

Of the books mentioned under sections 1-16 above, many are available in dual-language versions or in languages other than English. Information about these is available from, amongst others, the Bangladesh Resource and Multicultural Centre and Mantra Publishing, whose addresses are on page 72. Tamarind Books, also mentioned on page 72, provides posters, sequencing cards and jigsaws for several of its publications.

Checklist of books

ABC I Can Be by Verna Wilkins 10

Abena and the Rock by Verna Wilkins 16

All the Colours of the Earth by Sheila Hamanaka 1, 13, 14

Almaz and the Lion by Jane Kurtz 2, 8

Amazing Grace by Mary Hoffman 1, 3, 7

Arion and the Dolphin by Vikram Seth 4

Babu's Day by Mira Kapur 6, 8

Baby Just Like Me, A by Susan Winter 2, 7

Bad-Tempered Ladybird, The by Eric Carle 9

Balloon Detectives, The by Michael Jones 7

Balloon for Grandad, A by Nigel Gray 2, 8, 13

Ben Makes a Cake by Verna Wilkins 10

Beware Beware by Susan Hill 1, 13, 14,

Big Big Sea, The by Martin Waddell 2

Blodin the Beast by Michael Morpurgo 3

Boots for a Bridesmaid by Verna Wilkins 6, 10

Bringing the Rain to Kapiti Plain by Verna Aardema 5

Can I But a Slice of Sky by Grace Nichols 8

Dark, Dark Tale, A by Ruth Brown 6

Dave and the Tooth Fair by Verna Wilkins 6

Dem Bones by Bob Barner 11

Dreamstealer by Elaine Joseph 6

Each Peach Pear Plum by Alan Ahlberg 11

Eat Up, Gemma by Sarah Hayes, 12

Elmer by David McKee 9

Farmer Duck by Martin Waddell 9, 12

Finish the Story Dad by Nicola Smee 6

Fire Children, The by Eric Maddern 1, 5

Finished Being Four by Verna Wilkins 2

Five Things to Find Four by Verna Wilkins 16

Forest Whispers by Waltham Forest schools 1, 7

Frog Princess?, The by Pamela Mann 10, 11

Ganging Up by Alan Gibbons 2

Garden, The by Dyan Sheldon 6, 8

Gift for Gita, A by Rachna Gilmore 7

Girl Who Hated Books, The by Manjusha Pawagi 6, 7, 14

Golden Bear by Ruth Young 9

Grandpa Chatterji by Jamila Gavin 10

Grandpa's Handkerchief by Dorothy Clark 12

Guess How Much I Love You by Sam McBratney 2, 9

Hairy Tales and Nursery Crimes by Michael Rosen 13, 15

Handa's Surprise by Eileen Browne 8, 12, 14

Hue Boy by Rita Mitchell 2, 8,

Hunter, The by Paul Geraghty 4, 6, 8

I Din Do Nuttin by John Agard 7

I Don't Eat Toothpaste Any More by Karen King 2

In a Minute by Tony Bradman 2, 7

It Came From Outer Space by Tony Bradman 15

Jamaica and Brianna by Juanita Havil 2, 7, 10

Jamaica's Find by Juanita Havil 3, 7

Jeremiah in the Dark Woods by Alan Ahlberg 15

Just a Pile of Rice by Verna Wilkins 16

Kick-off by Hannah Cole 10

Kim's Magic Tree by Verna Wilkins 6

Kofi and the Butterflies by Sandra Horn 4, 8, 13

Lights for Gita by Rachna Gilmore 7

Lima's Hot Chilli by David Mills 2, 12

Lullaby for Daddy, A by Edward Smith 2

Make Hay While the Sun Shines by Shirley Hughes 11, 15

Many Rivers to Cross by Errol Lloyd 1, 7

Michael by Tony Bradman 15

Mother Eagle, Sister Sky by Chief Seattle 4, 5, 8

Moving by Michael Rosen 2, 9, 13

Moving Mango Tree, The by Zohra Jabeen 8

Mr Archimedes' Bath by Pamela Allen 9, 16,

Mufaro's Beautiful Daughters by John Steptoe 3, 8

Mum Can Fix It by Verna Wilkins 1

Night the Animals Fought, The by Jesus Zaton 4

Night Out by Vedasree Chadhuri 7

Nobody Owns the Sky by Reeve Lindbergh 3, 6, 7, 10

Oi Get Off Our Train by John Burningham 4, 6, 12

Old Woman and the Pumpkin, The by Michael Rosen 12

On the Way Home by Jill Murphy 6, 12

Over the Moon by Shirley Hughes 11, 15

Peace at Last by by Jill Murphy 2
People who Hugged the Trees, The
by Deborah Rose 3, 4, 8, 13, 14, 16
Present for Paul, A by Bernard Ashley 2, 7
Princess Smartypants by Babette Cole 10
Promise to the Sun, A by Tololwa Mollel 5

Radish Thief, The by Khodeja Khan 8
Rama and the Demon King by Jessica Southam 5, 11
Rata Pata Scata Fat by Phillis Gershator 6
Rose Blanche by Christophe Gallaz and
Roberto Innocenti 3, 13
Roses for Gita by Rachna Gilmore 7

Samira's Eid by Nasreen Aktar 7
Samira's Surprise by Nasreen Aktar 7
Savitri by Aaron Shepard 2, 5, 11
Send for Sohail by Sagir Richter 6, 7
So Much by Trish Cooke 2
Something on my Mind by Ronald Kay 1, 8
Something Rich and Strange by
William Shakespeare, edited by Gina Pollinger 11
Songolo by Niki Daly 2
Squeak-a-Lot by Martin Waddell 9, 12, 15
Shepherd Boy, The by Kim Lewis 1
Seashell Song, The by Susie Jenkin-Pearce
4, 6, 13
Shopping Basket, The by John Burningham 12
Snowball Rent, The by Verna Wilkins 16
Snowy Day, The by Jack Ezra Keats 6

Talking Walls, The by Margy Burns Knight 3, 8
Tar Beach by Faith Ringgold 6, 7, 10
Time to Get Up by Gill McLean 2
Tortoise's Dream by Joanna Troughton
1, 6, 9, 12, 14
Toyin Fay by Verna Wilkins 6
Turbulent Term of Tyke Tyler The by
Gene Kemp, 10
Turtle and the Island by Barbara Ker Wilson and
Frane Lessac 5

Very Best of Aesop's fables, The by
Margaret Clark 11
Very Hungry Caterpillar, The by Eric Carle 16
Village of Round and Square Houses, The by
Ann Grifalconi 5, 8

Whales' Song, The by Dyan Sheldon 6
Whale Boy by Michael Mansfield 4
Where's Gran? by David Rhys 2, 12
Whispering Cloth, The by Pegi Deitz Shea 3, 8,
Who Sank the Boat? by Pamala Allen 9, 14, 15, 16
Window by Jeannie Baker 14
Woman with the Pushchair by Steve Kaufman 7

You and Me Little Bear by Martin Waddell 2, 12
Yohance and the Dinosaurs by Alexis Obi
4, 6, 8, 13

Zoom by Istvan Banyai 14,15

To obtain copies of these books

As of December 1998 all the books in this list were in print and could be ordered from, for example, the Willesden Bookshop, Willesden Green Library Centre, 95 High Road, London NW10. Bilingual versions of many of them were available from the Bangladesh Resource and Multicultural Centre, address on page 72. Also on page 72 there are other useful addresses, including those of Bradford and Ilkley Community College, Mantra Publishing and Tamarind Books. The Young Book Trust is a useful source of information about newly published books.

Research on parental involvement

A research team led by staff at the Child Development and Learning Unit, University of London Institute of Education was commissioned to work in partnership with seven Brent primary schools to study and develop parental involvement. Questionnaires were returned from 115 teachers and 301 parents. Their responses were analysed according to a typology of five main kinds of possible involvement, and discussed at a range of meetings and inservice sessions. Broad principles underlying good practice were developed and agreed, and were used to plan specific projects and strategies which were incorporated into the schools' development plans. It was agreed that schools should have an ethos which:

- makes everyone feel that they are wanted and have a positive part to play in the school

- shows parents that they can always make their feelings, views and opinions known to the staff, and that these will be dealt with respectfully and seriously

- demonstrates that parents' linguistic, cultural and religious backgrounds are valued and seen as positive assets for the school

- shows that the school is an organic part of the community it serves, and so understands the concerns, aspirations and difficulties which the members of that community might face.

The features of such an ethos include:

- regular and effective communication

- willingness to share information with parents about their child and the school

- willingness to ask parents for advice about their child and to seek their views on key issues such as curriculum, child rearing and assessment

- working towards common goals, taking time to explain and listen carefully

- visibly displaying a liking for parents and respect for their feelings

- being approachable and open to negotiation

- sharing responsibility and a willingness to work together

- illustrating that the child is at the heart of the education provided and therefore that the care or family unit is all-important.

There is further information about the research on page 70.

Whole-school policies: review, reflection and renewal

Whole-school policies: review, reflection and renewal

Introductory notes

In this section of the book we provide some checklists which colleagues may find useful when reviewing their work. The lists can be used by individual teachers, or by pairs or teams of teachers, as they plan or reflect on their work. Also they may help to focus discussion in staff meetings and inset sessions, and in meetings between specialist EAL staff and mainstream staff.

There are five lists altogether. The first is concerned with practical classroom methods, and refers directly to earlier parts of the book. The others are about the wider context in which EAL teaching takes place, and on which its success to quite a large extent depends. They are to do with management and organisation (*list 2*), with partnership teaching (*list 3*), with working with new arrivals, including in particular children from refugee and asylum-seeking families (*list 4*), and with ensuring that all curriculum subjects take into account the multi-ethnic nature of British society (*list 5*).

1 Practical classroom methods

1.1 Planning

In our planning do we consciously and explicitly remind ourselves of a wide range of practical possibilities – including key visuals, writing frames and collaborative groupwork exercises – and do we consider not only language development but also academic development, cognitive development, and personal and social development? For example, do the lesson planning proformas in use at our school require us to bear such points in mind?

1.2 Intellectual challenge

Do we provide intellectually challenging tasks and problem-solving activities, for example tasks which involve classifying, comparing, selecting and evaluating, such that children's learning of English as an additional language is closely integrated with their general intellectual, academic and cognitive development?

1.3 Key visuals

Do we make use of visual material, including topic webs, flow charts, grids, matrices, graphs and diagrams, such that children's academic and cognitive development is not wholly dependent on their understanding of technical terms in English? (*Key visuals are described on pages 30-33*).

1.4 Hands as well as minds

Do we set practical and manipulative tasks, involving the hands as well as the brain, since these help to ensure that children's academic and cognitive development is not dependent on their language development alone, and since they make the meanings of new words and terminology easier to grasp?

1.5 Success

Do we employ activities which enable children to experience success, and which therefore build their self-confidence, self-esteem and motivation?

1.6 Writing

Do we provide focused assistance with writing, particularly non-fiction genres? For example, do we use writing frames? (*There are notes about writing frames on pages 42-45*).

1.7 Collaboration

Do we provide opportunities for structured discussion and collaborative groupwork, in order to promote not only intellectual understanding but also essential social and interpersonal skills, and to increase children's motivation? (*There are notes about collaborative groupwork on page 35-39*).

1.8 Groupings

Do we ensure that bilingual children are frequently able to interact and collaborate with native speakers of English?

1.9 Home languages

Do we encourage children to use their home language to support their cognitive and social development, and to develop their self-confidence, self-respect and motivation? Do we, for example, provide:

- opportunities to work in same-language groups and pairs and with bilingual staff and assistants?

- dual-language texts?

- tapes in home languages?

- access to dictionaries?

- access to bilingual glossaries and lists of keywords?

- opportunities for parents or members of the local community to work in the classroom with bilingual children?

Shahed

There is every reason to encourage beginners who are already literate to join in writing activities in the community language. Take the case of ten year old Shahed, who came from Iran with a high level of literacy in Farsi, but very little English. At the very beginning, his efforts were almost exclusively in Farsi, with just a short explanatory sentence in English and an illustration, to help explain what he had written to his teacher. As his confidence grew, he moved to dual-language texts, writing first in Farsi and then in English.

1.10 Vocabulary enrichment

Do we consciously aim to extend children' vocabulary? For example, by:

- teaching expressive adjectives and verbs?

- focusing on the specialist keywords and core concepts in curriculum subjects, and the correct and fluent use of these in writing?

- comparing and contrasting words in English with words in other languages?

- looking at words with similar sounds in puns and jokes?

- looking at metaphorical meanings, and working with proverbial sayings and famous quotations?

- encouraging children to enquire into the derivations of words, and at the ways in which words change in meaning or nuance over the years?

- encouraging attention to synonyms, and to nuances and gradations of meaning?

- looking at new words which have entered the English language over the last 20 or 30 years, and at their background and meaning?

- frequently encouraging children to consult a dictionary or a thesaurus?

1.11 Language awareness and knowledge about language

Do we make and take opportunities to encourage all children to have a lively interest in the nature of language, and in varieties of language within and between countries? For example:

- do children study differences between written and spoken English, between different registers, codes and dialects of spoken English, and between appropriate and inappropriate uses of English in a range of different situations?

- do children explore the meanings, derivations, synonyms and nuances of important words, both in English and in their home or community language?

- do children learn basic vocabulary (greetings, numbers, everyday objects and actions, etc) in a range of different languages?

- do children have opportunities to make bilingual books, and books in languages other than English?

- are there books in a variety of languages, and is a range of languages and scripts used in classroom displays and around the school?

- do we encourage or require children to think about their own learning of language, particularly their experience of becoming and being bilingual, for example by telling their own personal 'language stories' in speech or in writing?

- do we draw on the skills, perceptions and experience of staff (including administrative and support staff) who are themselves bilingual?

1. 12 Lesson observation

Do the proformas used for observation of lessons, for example by the head or other senior staff, or by inspectors or advisers from outside the school, require attention to the needs of bilingual learners? For example, do they refer to the items and possibilities listed here in paragraphs 1.2 – 1.11 above?

Our School, Our Languages – Adan, Sara and Omar, and their mums and dads

The parents of reception class children helped to write dual-language books about the school. Adan's dad wrote in Somali, Sara's mum wrote in Arabic, Omar's mum in Urdu. Other parents wrote in Portuguese, Gujerati and Serbo-Croat. The project was invaluable in creating good relationships with parents, and in developing the children's English as well as their pride in their own bilingualism.

---

2 Management and organisation

2.1 Language policy

Does our school's language policy emphasise that:

- language is central to a person's sense of identity and belonging?

- language development is essential for cognitive, academic and conceptual development?

- proficiency in standard English, particularly in writing, is essential for academic success?

- proficiency in standard English need not be, and should not be, achieved through devaluing or removing forms of language used in the home and community?

- mainstream class and subject teachers have responsibility for developing children's competence in formal academic English, both written and spoken?

- teaching English as an additional language requires a partnership between specialist EAL experts on the one hand and mainstream class teachers on the other?

2.2 Inset and staff development

When planning school-based training, or when considering attendance by staff at other training, do we bear in mind the needs of bilingual children? (Do we, for example, ensure that courses and inset events cover the main topics and concerns in this book?)

2.3 School development plan

Are issues to do with bilingualism and the progress and achievement of bilingual children prioritised in the current school development plan?

2.4 Resourcing

Are financial and staffing resources allocated, in accordance with the school development plan, to promote the progress and achievement of bilingual children?

2.5 Parental involvement

Do we take measures to ensure that ethnic minority parents are as involved proportionately as all other parents in the life of the school, for example as school governors and in meetings and events for parents? Do parents who are bilingual provide assistance in classrooms, for example for making dual-language books and notices and helping children to write in their mother tongue?

2.6 Racist bullying and name-calling

Do we have procedures, known to the support and administrative staff as well as the teachers, and also to children and their parents, for dealing with instances of racist bullying and name-calling in the playground, and on journeys to and from school?

2.7 Partnership teaching

Is training for all staff provided on the nature and procedures, and the benefits and advantages, of partnership teaching?

Listening

'The most effective schools were 'listening schools': schools which took time to talk with students and parents; which were prepared to consider and debate values as well as strategies; which took seriously the views students and parents offered and their own interpretations of school processes; and which used this learning to re-appraise, and where necessary change, their practices and to build a more inclusive curriculum.'

From *Making the Difference: teaching and learning strategies in successful multi-ethnic schools* by Maud Blair and Jill Bourne, Department for Education and Employment, 1998.

---

3 Partnership teaching

3.1 Definition and distinctions

Do we distinguish between support teaching and partnership teaching, and recognise that real partnership teaching involves two teachers taking joint responsibility for a lesson, with *both* involved in:

- planning and preparation?

- production of materials?

- considering the needs of 'targeted' children?

- considering also the needs of all other children in the class, including in particular those needing to develop their skills in written English?

- whole-class teaching?

- classroom management?

- recording each child's progress in English, both spoken and written, and in their home and community languages?

- review and evaluation?

- marking and record-keeping?

3.3 Advantages and benefits

Do we recognise that the advantages of partnership teaching include the following points:

- that two teachers working together are in principle more able to plan and run the kinds of lively, interactive groupwork and practical work which is the best context for promoting children's language development and conceptual development?

- that two teachers working together are in principle more able to engage in 'classroom action-research' – trying out new ideas, reflecting on their practice, and through such reflection improving their practical skills and expertise?

- that it is beneficial for all children in a class, not for the bilingual children only?

- that it contributes to the esteem in which EAL staff are held, both by mainstream teachers and by children, and is therefore valuable for their professional development and career prospects?

- that specialist EAL staff share their distinctive expertise with mainstream teachers?

3.4 Sharing

Do pairs of teachers who have engaged in partnership teaching have opportunities to share their reflections and experience with other members of staff and with the whole staff?

4 Welcoming new arrivals

4.1 Admission

When admitting a pupil who has recently arrived from another country, or shortly after admission, do we ensure that we have information about the pupil's linguistic and educational background, for example whether the pupil is literate in languages other than English?

4.2 Do we build home-school links with parents and carers, using bilingual staff if possible?

4.3 Do we ensure that parents and carers are invited to spend time at the school, including time in their child's classroom?

4.4 Are parents encouraged to explain concepts in the home language?

4.5 Does the induction period for the newly arrived pupil include measures such as the following:

- pairing the new arrival with a supportive friend or mentor?

- introduction to the lay-out of the school?

- sensitivity to dietary needs?

- use of multilingual labels?

- staff learning words in the pupil's home language?

- provision of home language support from peers or elder siblings?

- teaching key words and 'survival language'?

4.6 Do we provide sensitive opportunities for children from refugee and asylum-seeking families to explore and express their experience of dislocation and uprooting through art and literature?

4.7 Do we provide guidance to class teachers on the early stages of learning English as an additional language? For example:

- the nature of the 'silent period' when a child first arrives?

- the importance of assessing a child's understanding of science and mathematics without depending inappropriately on English?

- the importance of making notes to record the child's progress?

- the importance of interaction with other children, both in English and in the child's home language?

The New Arrival – researching needs and providing support

A team of teachers looked at their school's arrangements for welcoming new children. They interviewed staff, asked children to write and discuss stories about their own memories, and observed closely a number of children who had just arrived. On the basis of these enquiries they made a series of practical recommendations for improvements, devised a form entitled 'Help us to know your child' for use with parents, and compiled a handbook of guidance for staff. The five questions used for discussion with children were:

1 Do you remember something that made you happy when you were first at the school?
2 Do you remember something that made you sad when you were first at school?
3 What is the first piece of work you remember doing?
4 Do you remember your first day at school? How did it feel?
5 What sort of things could be changed around the school to help the children who speak no English?

---

5   Curriculum for a just and inclusive society

In every curriculum subject do we take opportunities to reflect and support cultural diversity amongst children, and to teach about equality and fairness? Do we, for example, frequently refer to and stress:

- cultural, ethnic and religious diversity, both in Britain and in the wider world?

- but also commonalities – the qualities, concerns and aspirations which all human beings have in common?

- the nature and dynamics of racism, discrimination and prejudice?

- practical ways of addressing discrimination and prejudice, in personal, local and national affairs?

In more detail, do we take opportunities to mention, include or emphasise:

5.1 Art

- excellence in a range of different cultural traditions, and in cross-cultural borrowings and influences?

- common elements, concerns and strivings in different traditions, reflecting shared human values?

- visiting artists – painters, photographers, potters, sculptors, printmakers – from a range of cultures and traditions?

- artistic expression to explore social and political issues, and children's own sense of personal and cultural identity?

5.2 English and drama

- fiction, drama and poetry from a range of genres, times and places, exploring values and concerns which all human beings have in common?

- recognition of bias in literature and the media, and questioning of stereotypes?

- the importance of oracy, the importance of standard English, the differences between spoken and written English, the nature of registers and codes?

- the use of language and literature to explore social and political issues, and personal and cultural identity?

5.3 Geography

- differences and commonalities in humankind's relationship with the physical environment?

- global connections and interdependence?

- avoidance of negative images of Third World countries?

- migration, population movement and settlement as recurring features of human experience?

5.4 History

- differing perceptions of, and narratives about, the same event?

- British history within a world perspective, related to events in other countries?

- key political concepts, for example democracy, rule of law, rights and obligations, equality, justice?

- study of local heritage, neighbourhood and community in such a way as to support all children's sense of personal identity and personal history?

5.5 Mathematics

- mathematics as a universal human language, used in all cultures and societies?

- tasks, problems, materials and activities which reflect the multi-ethnic and multi-cultural nature of modern societies?

- the use of mathematics in analysing social, economic and political affairs?

- links with other subjects, to develop children's knowledge of themselves, their relationships and the wider world?

5.6 Modern Foreign Languages

- cultural, social and historical contexts?

- contrasts and comparisons between different languages, and borrowings and influences?

- bilingualism and multilingualism seen as widespread throughout the world?

- open and enquiring attitudes towards diversity within and between languages?

5.7 Music

- excellence and high achievement in a range of different cultural traditions, and in cross-cultural borrowings and influences?

- common elements, concerns and strivings in different traditions, and common aesthetic values and meanings?

- visiting musicians from a range of backgrounds and traditions?

- the use of music to explore aspects of personal identity, and social problems and issues?

5.8 Physical Education

- games and sport as universal human activities?

- cooperation and sensitivity, fair play and respect, acceptance of rules and decisions, handling of success and failure?

- dance used as a medium for exploring aspects of personal identity, and social and political issues?

- name-calling and racial abuse unacceptable in team games, including fixtures with other schools, as well as in all other aspects of school life?

5.9 Personal, social and health education

- support for a range of personal and cultural identities amongst children and parents?

- concepts of discrimination, prejudice, exclusion, harassment, injustice?

- listening to and taking account of children's own perceptions, experiences and concerns?

- reflection on events in the school itself, including any bullying and racist name-calling, and in the local neighbourhood, and support and assistance as appropriate for children themselves to act as mediators?

5.10 Religious education and collective worship

- common elements, concerns and values in different religious traditions?

- cultural, national and ethnic diversity within each religion?

- critical studies of media misrepresentations and stereotypes, and of negative stereotypes in wider society?

- teachings and stories about tolerance, fairness, management and resolution of conflict, reconciliation?

5.11 Science

- processes of observing, hypothesising, rationality and testing universal throughout all cultures?

- resources, materials and activities which reflect the multi-ethnic and multicultural nature of modern societies?

- the use of scientific method in analysing social, economic and political affairs?

- no scientific basis for supposing that the human species is divided into separate races?

5.12 Technology, including information and communications technology

- common elements in human experience across cultures and countries, for example shelter, transport, food preparation?

- resources, tasks and activities reflecting the multi-ethnic nature of modern societies?

- avoidance of negative images of Third World countries?

- use of ICT to explore social and political issues, and aspects of personal and cultural identity

Many of the points in this list are derived from *Equality Assurance in Schools: quality, identity, society*, first published by the Runnymede Trust in 1993 (see Bibliography, page 71).

References, bibliography and useful addresses

References

(Please note: all schools mentioned in these references are in the London Borough of Brent.)

Becoming bilingual *(pages 11-22)*

The descriptions of Thaeba and Mohammed were originally written by Frank Williams, at Gladstone Park School. The conversation with Usha and Lena was conducted and transcribed by Chris Raeside. Usha and Lena were students at John Kelly Girls' Technology College, as was Andreia. For information about the languages spoken by these children and young people, see the books in the bibliography by Edwards and Katzner. On bilingualism see the book by Alladina and the introduction to the book by Gibbons.

Routes for bilingual learners: general background

For more discussion of the theories underlying the ideas in this part of the book, see the works by Jim Cummins, Pauline Gibbons and Josie Levine in the bibliography. Specifically on key visuals, see the book by Steve Cooke. On writing frames, the books by Maureen Lewis and David Wray. On ways with words, the book by Norah McWilliam.

Decision trees *(page 31)*

The teachers responsible for this work were Karen Tombs and Alison Hicks, Salusbury School, supported by Charmian Kenner working as consultant.

Structure and sequence grid *(page 32)*

The matrix activity using Grandpa's Handkerchief was developed by Aparna Mukherjee, Wembley Manor Infants School.

Piecing the pattern together *(page 38)*

The teachers who devised this exercise were Sue Browne and Ruquia Sheikh, Sudbury Junior School.

The labours of Heracles *(page 39)*

The teachers were Nicky Clark and Jo Talbot, Roe Green Junior School.

The water cycle *(page 36)*

The teachers were Sarah Jane Moody, Abi Rosen and John Vickers, Uxendon Manor Primary School.

Le mot juste *(page 47)*

The teachers were Jonathan Binns and Sandra Kelly, Preston Park Primary School.

Planning and self-review *(pages 59-68)*

This section of the book derives in part from *Equality Assurance in Schools*, first published by the Runnymede Trust in 1993, as developed by the Insted educational consultancy in 1996-1998 in collaboration with several local education authorities, including in particular Hounslow and Staffordshire as well as Brent.

Research on parental involvement *(page 58)*

The research took place between September 1996 and March 1997 as part of an inset programme in Brent and was directed by Dr Iram Siraj-Blatchford, assisted by Liz Brooker and Orla Cronin, of the Child Development and Learning Unit, University of London Institute of Education.

Our school, our languages *(page 63)*

The teacher was Cheryl Esbrand, Park Lane School.

The new arrival *(page 66)*

The teachers involved in this enquiry were Tony Butler, Miles Chester and Neelam Malik, Kensal Rise School. The subsequent pack for mainstream colleagues was compiled by Kusum Pal.

Bibliography

Alladina, Safder (1995) *Being Bilingual: a guide for parents, teachers and young people*, Trentham Books.

Barrs, Myra et al (1990) *Patterns of Learning: the primary language record and the national curriculum*, Centre for Language in Primary Education.

Blair, Maud and Bourne, Jill et al (1998) *Making the Difference: teaching and learning strategies in successful multi-ethnic schools*, Department for Education and Employment.

Clegg, John ed (1996) *Mainstreaming ESL: case studies in integrating ESL students into the mainstream classroom*, Multilingual Matters.

Cooke, Steve (1997) *Collaborative Learning Activities in the Classroom: designing inclusive materials for learning and language development*, Resource Centre for Multicultural Education, Leicester

Crystal, David (1998) *Language Play*, Penguin.

Cummins, Jim (1997) *Negotiating Identities: education for empowerment in a diverse society*, Trentham Books.

Edwards, Viv (1996) *The Other Languages: a guide to multilingual classrooms, Reading and Language Information Centre*, University of Reading.

Fitzpatrick, Finbarré (1994) *The Linguistic Background of ESL*, Department of Teaching Studies, Bradford and Ilkley Community College.

Gibbons, Pauline (1991) *Learning to Learn in a Second Language*, Primary English Teaching Association, Australia.

Gravelle, Maggie (1996) *Supporting Bilingual Learners in Schools*, Trentham Books.

Katzner, Kenneth (1977, revised 1986) *The Languages of the World*, Routledge.

Levine, Josie (1996) *Developing Pedagogies in the Multilingual Classroom*, Trentham Books.

Language and Curriculum Access Service (1995) *Making Progress: teaching and assessment in the multilingual classroom*, London Borough of Enfield.

Language and Curriculum Access Service (1997) *Scaffolding learning in the multilingual classroom*, London Borough of Enfield.

Lewis, Maureen and Wray, David (1997) *Writing Frames: scaffolding children's writing in a range of genres*, Reading and Language Information Centre, University of Reading.

Lewis, Maureen and Wray, David (1997) *Writing Across the Curriculum: frames to support learning*, Reading and Language Information Centre, University of Reading.

Leung, Constant and Cable, Carrie, eds, (1997) *English as an Additional Language: changing perspectives*, National Association for Language Development in the Curriculum (NALDIC).

McWilliam, Norah (1998) *What's in a Word? – vocabulary development in multilingual classrooms*, Trentham Books.

Multilingual Matters (1995) *Building Bridges: multilingual resources for children*, University of Reading.

Runnymede Trust (1993) *Equality Assurance in Schools: quality, identity, society*, Runnymede Trust with Trentham Books.

School Curriculum and Assessment Authority (1996) *Teaching English as an Additional Language: new perspectives*, SCAA Publications.

School Curriculum and Assessment Authority (1996) *Teaching English as an Additional Language: a framework for policy*, SCAA Publications.

Useful addresses and contacts

Bangladesh Resource and Multicultural Book Centre, 23-25 Hessel Street, London E1 2LR. Tel 0171 488 4243.

Brent Language Service, Centre for Staff Development, Brentfield Road, London NW10 8HE. Tel 0181 937 3370.

Centre for Language in Primary Education, Webber Row, London SE1 8QW. Tel 0171 633 0840.

Insted Ltd, The Old School, Kilburn Park Road, London NW6 5XA. Tel 0171 372 0965.

Mantra Publishing, 5 Alexandra Grove, London N12 8NU. Tel 0181 445 5123.

Multilingual Matters, Frankfurt Lodge, Clevedon Hall, Victoria Road, Clevedon, Somerset BS21 7SJ.

National Association for Language Development in the Curriculum (NALDIC), South West Herts LCSC, Holywell School Site, Tolpits Lane, Watford WD1 8NT. Tel 0192 322 5130.

Partnership Publishing, Department of Teaching Studies, Bradford and Ilkley Community College, Great Horton Road, Bradford BD7 1AY. Tel 0127 475 3464.

Reading and Language Information Centre, University of Reading, Bulmershe Court, Earley, Reading RG6 1HY. Tel 0118 931 8820.

Resource Centre for Multicultural Education, Forest Lodge Education Centre, Charnor Road, Leicester LE3 6LH. Tel 0116 231 3399.

Runnymede Trust, 133 Aldersgate Street, London EC1A 4JA. Tel 0171 600 9666.

Tamarind Books, Box 296, Camberley, Surrey GU15 4WD. Tel 0127 668 3979.

Trentham Books, Westview House, 734 London Road, Oakhill, Stoke-on-Trent, ST4 5NP. Tel 01782 745567, fax: 01782 745553.

Young Book Trust, Book House, 45 East Hill, London SW18 2QZ.